BEING THE BELIEVING 2.0

Thomas McCracken

sermonto**book**
.com

Sermon To Book
www.sermontobook.com

Being the Believing 2.0 / Thomas McCracken
ISBN-13: 978-1-945793-91-2

This book is dedicated to all of the genuine believers who have lived before God with a heart of integrity and have impacted my life greatly. Standing tall among these "giants of the faith" is my wife of twenty-nine years. While others had told me of Christianity, she was the first to show me real faith lived out. Laurie McCracken was the first person in my life who demonstrated what Being the Believing really was, and because of that, I became a follower of Jesus Christ and discovered for myself the joy of Being the Believing.

CONTENTS

Foreword
by Jonathan Falwell

One of the primary callings of any pastor is to lead the people whom he has the privilege of pastoring into a deeper relationship with Christ. It is not enough for a pastor to simply inform them of the message of the gospel, though certainly this is key. Pastors have a strong desire, and a God-given command, to help people grow in their faith.

Jesus gave us our marching orders in no uncertain terms. He said, "Go into all the world and proclaim the gospel" (Mark 16:15). He told us to "make disciples of all nations" (Matthew 28:19) and that we will be His witnesses in "Jerusalem and in all Judea and Samaria, and to the end of the earth" (Acts 1:8). Those are not suggestions; they are commands. While it is clear that gospel proclamation is vital, it is likewise clear that making disciples is vital.

This is why I am so excited about this book, *Being the Believing*, by Pastor Tom McCracken. His passion and desire to help people become all that God intended is evident. And there is no greater place in all the world to learn how to live out our faith than from the teachings of Christ, and more specifically, the Beatitudes. Tom has spent a great deal of time praying over each of the eight blessings and encouragements given by Christ to mankind and, as a result, shares his heart in these pages.

Jesus wants each of us to understand how important it is to live out our faith on a daily basis. He wants us to not only embrace the Great Commission but the Great Commandment. Jesus, when asked about the greatest commandment, said it is to "love the Lord your God with all your heart and with all your soul and with all your mind. … And a second is like it: You shall love your neighbor as yourself" (Matthew 22:37, 39). That is why this book is so important and so‘timely.

This book will help you to understand why we must seek God's Word and way in our lives and embrace His way of living. In doing so, we will strengthen our daily walk and prepare for any situation that might come our way. As Pastor Tom so eloquently writes, it's not nearly enough that we *do good;* we must *be good.* And there is no possibility of truly "being good" unless we are fully immersed in the deeper Christian life that Christ intends.

As you read this book, determine to not only read the words on the page but let them truly sink into your heart. Allow the meaning behind each of the Beatitudes to take root in your mind. Make the commitment that this won't be just another book you read. Let it be the catalyst for you to apply God's desire and plan in your life. This is what Jesus intended when He gave those eight great encouragements.

In Acts 1:8, we are told by Christ, "But you will receive power when the Holy Spirit has come upon you, and you will be my witnesses in Jerusalem and in all Judea and Samaria, and to the end of the earth." In this verse, we find a promise and a command. First, Jesus promises that we *shall* receive power. And then, we are commanded that we *will* be witnesses. *Being the Believing* will teach you how to use that power and fulfill that command to change the world.

Jonathan Falwell
Senior Pastor of Thomas Road Baptist Church, Lynchburg, Virginia

INTRODUCTION

Being the Believing

There is a big difference between doing good and being good. And the fact that many people do not know that difference is why there are so many people feeling unloved, living in a world that is unable to satisfy.

Like many people, I grew up in an environment of works-based relationships, which led to years of being disillusioned, dissatisfied, and dysfunctional. I was frustrated and hopeless. When I was four years old, my dad had an affair that ultimately led to my parents getting divorced. Although I did not have the maturity to articulate my feelings, I can tell you that even at that young age, I believed that I was at fault. I thought that perhaps if I were a better kid, my dad would not have walked out of my life to start another family.

A few years later, my mom started dating a new man. I am told that the first time her boyfriend came over to meet me, I rushed to the door, hugged his legs, and asked, "Are you going to be my new daddy?" From that point on, I was determined to do everything in my power to please him, to work so hard that he would never have a reason to leave me like my biological dad did.

Eventually, my mom married this man, and I quickly discovered that he was the smartest, strongest, and most talented man in my world. The bar was set high in this works-based relationship! My new dad was a third-degree black belt in taekwondo, so I decided that I would earn his love by taking karate lessons. Unfortunately, I was the clumsiest kid in the world—the one who often fell down putting on his pants and occasionally fell going up the stairs! During one karate lesson, I attempted to do a round-house kick that I had seen in a movie, only to face-plant on the mat in front of all my classmates. I was so embarrassed that I quit studying karate.

My stepdad was also an Eagle Scout, so I joined the Cub Scouts and decided to work my way through Boy Scouts with the goal of achieving the same rank. After a few months, our Cubmaster called my parents for a meeting to discuss my poor behavior. That put an end to my Scouting career.

My stepdad was also a bicycle racer—at one point, he was even sponsored by 7-Eleven. One day, I visited his bike workshop and asked if he would train me. At my first race, as I waited with the group for the horn to blow, I proudly looked to the sidelines to see my mom and stepdad cheering me on. I think I made it one mile into the five-mile race before I pulled off to the side of the road and leaned my bike against a tree, struggling to catch my breath. I will never forget that old Chevrolet Chevet pulling over, my stepdad loading my bike on the rack, and the three of us driving home in complete silence as I sat in the back seat, defeated once again.

In a world where doing good was rewarded, my trophy shelf remained empty.

Since my stepdad held a master's degree from Penn State University in acoustical consulting, my last effort was to excel academically. No matter how hard I tried, report card after report card was sent home with consistent D's and the occasional C, which were met with constant groundings and reprimands. After a fifth-grade parent-teacher conference confirmed to me that I was worthless, I gave up on that path as well. I realized I would never be able to work hard enough to win my stepdad's approval, acceptance, or applause.

Things didn't get any better. Over the years, counselors lamented that I would never amount to anything. Teachers reviewed my work and declared that I was no good. Adults discounted me as worthless, and other children shunned me as damaged goods. In a world where *doing good* was rewarded, my trophy shelf remained empty.

I wasted many years of my life trying to *do good* to please those around me: my parents, family, counselors, teachers, bosses, and friends. All of these folks came at me from different directions and perspectives, their well-intentioned voices echoing the same sentiment: "Tom, *do good!*" And for many years, I felt like a failure for not living up to that expectation. I never dreamed that one day I could *be* good.

Again, there is a big difference between *doing good* and *being good.* That difference is found in the Beatitudes.

You are wasting your time if you are trying to *do good* without *being good* first. You will fail. That is the beauty of the Beatitudes, that God has given us all that we need, not to *do good,* but to *be good.* And that is what this book is all about.

I am so excited that you have decided to make the investment and take the time to join me in this journey through the Beatitudes. I pray that after reading this book, you will have the confidence and assurance that comes from an intimate relationship with God through Jesus Christ. I pray that you will find, as I did, the joy that comes from understanding the difference between *doing good* and *being good.*

Please take full advantage of the discussion questions at the end of each chapter and the links to my videos that dig a little deeper into each of the Beatitudes. I also encourage you to visit my website, www.beingthebelieving.com, where you can share your story, ask me questions, purchase additional resources, and network with other believers.

CHAPTER ONE

From Rags to Riches
with Dreama Denver

Seeing the crowds, he went up on the mountain, and when he sat down, his disciples came to him. And he opened his mouth and taught them, saying: Blessed are the poor in spirit, for theirs is the kingdom of heaven.
—Matthew 5:1–3

The first word of Matthew 5:1, "seeing," has captivated me both theologically and personally, as does Hebrews 1:1, which says, "Long ago, at many times and in many ways, God *spoke* to our fathers by the prophets" (emphasis added). What an amazing event! God did not have to speak. He was not lonely; He did not need a new friend. He was not incomplete without us, and we certainly did not deserve to hear the voice of Almighty God. Yet He chose to speak anyway. And here, we find that God sees us.

To understand the significance of Jesus "seeing" the crowds, we must delve into the theology behind this word.

In this simple yet profound statement, the apostle Matthew is comparing the Old Testament Moses to the New Testament Christ. He is saying that just as Moses, the deliverer of the nation of Israel, went up a mountain (Exodus 19:3) and sat down (Deuteronomy 9:9), Jesus Christ, the better Deliverer, went up a mountain and sat down (Matthew 5:1). Just as Moses gave a law that would be binding, Jesus gave liberty that would be freeing. In other words, Moses was concerned with leading his people to *do good,* while Jesus offered the power to *be good.*

Moses was concerned with leading his people to do good, while Jesus offered the power to be good.

One of my favorite arguments, from C.S. Lewis in his book *Mere Christianity,* asked if Jesus was a liar, lunatic, or Lord.[1] To believe that Jesus Christ was more than a prophet, miracle worker, teacher, healer, or priest is to believe that He is the risen and living Savior, seated before the disciples and crowds, speaking to humanity through the Sermon on the Mount. By comparing Moses to Christ, Matthew seeks to prove that the words of Jesus carry divine authority because He is the better Moses.

Now, having established that Jesus is the Messiah prophesied in the Old Testament, we can take a look at this word "seeing." As I stated earlier, this word has captivated me both theologically and personally. To know that God sees *us*, what with everything He has going on in the universe, is compelling to say the least.

Even more profound is the understanding that the Greek word in this passage for "see," *eido*, implies a deep knowledge of the unseen.[2] In other words, only God has the unique, supernatural ability to see the *real* you, the you that is never shared with anyone else. The deep-rooted pain, the past hurts, the emotional scars, the restless nights, the struggles with sin, your hopes and dreams, your fears and doubts, and your worries and anxieties— God sees *that* you!

Saved by Our Shepherd

It has been said that people only know as much about us as we let them, unless something inadvertently slips out. The people around you do not have access to the full, unadulterated *real* you. If we were totally open, honest, and transparent to those around us about our past and what we think and how we feel, the rooms of our lives would be mostly empty. However, God does have access to the *real* you. He "sees" you, and He has still chosen to remain in your room.

*There are 238 countries on this planet and more than 17,000 people groups, representing more than seven billion people, yet God sees **you**.*

There are 238 countries on this planet and more than 17,000 people groups, representing more than seven billion people, yet God sees *you*.[3] And with God, to *see* you is to *know* you. In fact, God knows you better than anyone, yet chooses to love you more than everyone! The theological implications captivate me, and the personal ramifications encourage me.

In Exodus 2, we are introduced to a man named Moses. After forty years of living in Pharaoh's house, receiving a world-class education, and enjoying every kind of luxury, Moses experienced a turning point in his life when he witnessed the abuse of a fellow Israelite at the hands of an Egyptian (Acts 7:20–24). Moses made a decision: he struck down and killed the Egyptian who was beating a fellow Hebrew. Because of his crime, Pharaoh sought to kill Moses, so Moses fled to the wilderness in fear for his life.

By the time Moses went up to the mountain of God and approached the burning bush, he had a heavy heart (Exodus 3). His people were slaves under the sadistic hands of the Egyptian taskmasters and ruled by the pagan Pharaoh.

Moses himself had spent many years on the back side of the wilderness, struggling through guilt, shame, regret, fear, and lack of purpose. I am sure he felt that nobody cared, that he was all alone, and that God did not see what was going on. After forty years of silence, in answer to his tormented heart, the Lord said, "I have surely *seen* the affliction of my people who are in Egypt and have heard their cry because of their taskmasters. I *know* their sufferings" (Exodus 3:7, emphasis added). Don't miss this, as for God to see you is for God to know you, and for God to know you is for God to care about you.

When we really understand that God sees us, knows us, cares about us, and is able to help us, our natural response is to position ourselves as close to Him as possible.

Some people see but don't care, others care but don't see, and still others don't see or care. It's life changing to know that God both sees and cares. Jesus' life and ministry demonstrates this. No wonder Matthew 5:1 concludes with: "…his disciples came to him."

Jesus is often referred to as the Good Shepherd. When one of the flock places itself in danger by wandering away, a shepherd will undertake measures to correct it, keeping it close. For its part, the errant sheep learns to stay close and depend on the shepherd. One could look out at a fold of a hundred sheep and determine which ones used to be disobedient: the ones that position themselves as close as possible to the shepherd whom they identify as their source of care and protection.

When we really understand that God sees us, knows us, cares about us, and is able to help us, our natural response is to position ourselves as close to Him as possible. That's why, since my salvation about three decades ago, I can't get enough of my God. Any time His Word is being taught and preached or His people are meeting, fellowshipping, praying, or serving, I am right in the middle of the action!

I want to position myself as close to the Shepherd as I can, knowing He is the source of my care and protection.

Please believe that the God of the universe sees, cares, and is able and willing to help us. And because He cares, He has earned the right to our attention. Matthew records in Matthew 5:2, "And [Jesus] opened his mouth and taught them." According to Matthew 4:16, the people had been dwelling in darkness and living in the shadow of death. But once Jesus called them to Himself, all of that changed. They were now drawn to the light, rescued from their depravity, and compelled to listen to the voice of God because of the invitation to His love.

Boy, doesn't that sound like us? Many people today are living in spiritual darkness, doing life their way and enjoying all that the world has to offer. They are controlled by their feelings and emotions, yielding to sin. They are isolated, overwhelmed, and defeated. And rightfully so, for when we choose the world over Jesus, the Bible says that we are children of wrath destined to spend an eternity in hell, separated from the love of God forever (Ephesians 2:1–3; Romans 6:23). But then God "gave his only Son, that whoever believes in him should not perish but have eternal life" (John 3:16).

Jesus offers to rescue us from our depravity, save us by His sacrifice, redeem us through His grace, and shower us with His blessings by compelling us to listen to His voice because of His love. He offers to bring us from rags to riches. Based on His love displayed on the cross, backed by the power of His resurrection three days later, I would say that He has earned the right to our attention.

In Deuteronomy 18:15, Moses writes, "The LORD your God will raise up for you a prophet like me from among you, from your brothers—it is to him you shall *listen*" (emphasis added). Who was Moses speaking of? He was speaking of Jesus Christ.

Satisfied and Approved

In Matthew 5:3, Jesus states, "Blessed are the poor in spirit, for theirs is the kingdom of heaven." He is saying that blessed are those who recognize their desperate situation and are willing to listen to the message of love He offers.

Now let me draw your attention to the word "blessed" and first explain what this word does not mean.

Being "blessed" does not refer to happiness that is tethered to feelings and emotions, which are anchored to external situations. Many people anchor their happiness to the things of this world. These folks are happy when the sun is shining and sad when it is raining. They are happy when there is money in the bank but discouraged when their account runs dry. They are happy when their health, relationships, and jobs are all in good condition but devastated when they receive bad news from the doctor, have a conflict with their spouse, or lose their job. There has to be more to life than simply surviving, grinding through each week, living paycheck to paycheck, and basing how we feel on what we have. Friends, the problem with attaching our happiness to feelings and emotions is that feelings and emotions change every day and with every circumstance.

If "blessed" here does not refer to happiness that's tethered to fluctuating emotions and changeable circumstances, what does this word mean? The word *blessed* speaks of an inner, complete satisfaction that is tethered to salvation in Christ and is not subject to changing emotion, fear, or circumstances. It is an inner joy that is established in God. It's not given by this world, so it can't be taken by this world. In the Greek language, the word *blessed*, which is *makarios*, can simply mean "approved by God."[4]

So, we could read verse 3 thusly: "Approved by God are the poor in spirit, for theirs is the kingdom of heaven."

Like Beggars and Worms

After the apostle Matthew fixes our attention on the One worthy of our attention, we find that the very first thing Jesus says to His new disciples, after He calls them to follow Him in Matthew 4:19, is "Blessed are the poor in spirit" (Matthew 5:3).

"Poor in spirit" presents some more interesting Greek interpretations, but again, let me start by clarifying what the phrase does not mean.

First, "poor in spirit" does not mean that you have no value. God does not bless someone because they need more value, as all of humanity has value in His eyes. In speaking of God's relationship to humanity, the prophet Zephaniah declares, "The LORD your God is in your midst, a mighty one who will save; he will rejoice over you with gladness; he will quiet you by his love; he will exult over you with loud singing" (Zephaniah 3:17).

In a culture that looks to social media as a source for approval, acceptance, validation, and love, many people have found themselves with an insatiable void in their lives. Additionally, there are many who face a constant battle with the voices on the inside, which clamor that their life has no value and are seemingly confirmed by the voices from the outside. Don't you dare believe that lie! You are a creation of the living God, and He loves you with an everlasting love. The Bible says that you were created in His image and in His likeness (Genesis 1:27) and that you were formed and fashioned while you were in your mother's womb (Psalm 139:13). When you start viewing your life through the One who created you, that void will be filled with unspeakable love.

Furthermore, there is nothing you can do to make God love you any more than He already does, and there is nothing you can do to make God love you any less. He is in love with you!

Second, being "poor in spirit" is not speaking of someone who takes great pride in their humility. In his book on the Sermon on the Mount, R. Kent Hughes shares a story of Martyn Lloyd-Jones, the minister of Westminster Chapel in London. Lloyd-Jones tells of meeting a man who could be described as "poor in spirit" on one of his preaching missions.

> When Dr. Lloyd-Jones arrived at a train station, a man asked for the minister's suitcase and, in fact, almost ripped it from his hand, saying, "I am a deacon in the church where you are preaching tomorrow. You know, I am a mere nobody, a very unimportant man. Really. I do not count; I am not a great man in the church; I am just

one of those men who carry the bag for the minister." Lloyd-Jones observes, "He was anxious that I should know what a humble man he was, how 'poor in spirit.' Yet by his anxiety to make it known, he was denying the very thing he was trying to establish."[5]

The blessing of being poor in spirit is not speaking of someone who takes great pride in their perceived humility.

Third, being "poor in spirit" does not mean that you have no money and are destined to poverty. For the apostle Peter declared, "Truly I understand that God shows no partiality" (Acts 10:34). God does not approve those who live in a cardboard box on a dirt floor any more than He does the owner of a mansion in Beverly Hills. He loves every one of us the same, for He died for us all the same. So, the blessing of being poor in spirit is not speaking of a lack of material possessions.

If this word "poor" is not connected to value, showy humility, or money, what does it mean? The Greek word for "poor," *ptochos*, employed here actually means to cower and cringe like a beggar.[6]

Here is a scriptural example that helps us understand this word. Luke 16:19–21 says, "There was a rich man who was clothed in purple and fine linen and who feasted sumptuously every day. And at his gate was laid a *poor* man named Lazarus, covered with sores, who desired to be fed with what fell from the rich man's table. Moreover, even the dogs came and licked his sores" (emphasis added).

Paul was spot-on when he described himself as the foremost of sinners.

This poor man had no control over his life. He was so bankrupt that he was completely dependent upon the help of others to survive. He was so desperately poor that the only way he could obtain even a crumb for sustenance was to acknowledge his beggarly state and receive whatever help was offered. When we teach, read, or even preach through this account in Luke, we often focus on our role in helping this poor man. In fact, I preached a message a couple of years ago (titled "Who Has God Laid at Your Gate?") that outlined our need to love and care for those around us by being gospel driven. However, there is another way to view this text, and it is connected to Matthew 5:3 through the word *ptochos* in the Greek language.

Though this information may wound your pride a bit, the word "poor" in Luke 16, which is used to describe a sore-ridden, disease-carrying, poorer-than-poor reproach to society, is the same word used in Matthew 5:3. So Matthew 5:3 could say, "Approved of God are those who cower and cringe like a beggar: the pitiful, inferior, and worthless, theirs is the kingdom of heaven."

One of the old Christian hymns, "Rock of Ages", echoes this sentiment with words like, "Nothing in my hand I bring, simply to the cross I cling."[7]

The apostle Peter had it right when he declared, "Depart from me, for I am a sinful man, O Lord" (Luke 5:8).

And the apostle Paul was spot-on when he described himself as the foremost of sinners (1 Timothy 1:15).

The prophet Isaiah knew this truth when he cried, "Woe is me! For I am lost; for I am a man of unclean lips" (Isaiah 6:5).

The mighty Gideon, who delivered Israel from a vast army with just three hundred men, acknowledged to God, "I am the least in my father's house" (Judges 6:15).

You must come to the place where you believe, really and truly believe, that you are a wretched, miserable, beggarly-poor, sinning worm that needs someone outside of you and bigger than you to help and rescue you.

The Isaac Watts hymn written in 1885, "At the Cross," had it right when the stanza was sung, "Would He devote that sacred head, for such a *worm* as I." Newer hymnals, unfortunately, have replaced the words "for such a *worm* as I" with "for such a *sinner* as I," or even worse, "for such a *one* as I."[8] In our current American church culture where self-esteem prevails, we don't like anything that may damage our precious self-image.

King David, a man after God's own heart, would not have sung "for such a one as I," for he had no problem acknowledging his worm-like status when he declared in Psalm 22:6, "I am a worm and not a man."

The great William Carey, a Baptist missionary in the 1700s and 1800s who was known as the father of modern missions, had no issue with this word either, for on his gravestone are the words, "A wretched, poor, and helpless worm, on Thy kind arms I fall."[9]

You must come to the place where you believe, really and truly believe, that you are a wretched, miserable, beggarly-poor, sinning worm that needs someone outside of you and bigger than you to help and rescue you.

We must embrace the formula found in Isaiah 41:13–14: "For I, the LORD your God, hold your right hand; it is I who say to you, 'Fear not, I am the one who helps you.' Fear not, you *worm* Jacob, you men of Israel! I am the one who helps you, declares the LORD; your Redeemer is the Holy One of Israel."

From Spiritual Poverty to the Gift of Grace

Every recovery program designed to promote change starts with an acknowledgement and admission, birthed from introspection, that change is necessary. That is the crux of this first Beatitude, "Blessed are the poor in spirit, for theirs is the kingdom of heaven" (Matthew 5:3). Those who seek acceptance and approval from God must start their spiritual journey by taking that first step of recognizing and acknowledging their spiritual poverty—or simply put, their *need* for God. The above writers who admitted their worm-like status were taking that first step. They were recognizing their sinful state and enjoying the gift of acceptance, thus inheriting "the kingdom of heaven."

Last year, I got to meet and befriend someone who has a very special connection to my childhood: Dreama Denver. Dreama is the widow of Bob Denver, who played Gilligan on *Gilligan's Island*, a television show from the 1960s. My grandfather and I would watch that show together every week—one of the few things that bridged our generation gap was laughter. When I met Dreama, I was quick to point out how much her husband's show meant to me. Since we have become closer, I now realize that Dreama has her own powerful rags-to-riches story to tell, and I want to share that with you, in her own words:

> As a young woman, I was an actress, primarily a stage actress. For fourteen years, I worked nonstop all over the U.S. and Canada, performing with well-known names—Sal Mineo, Robert Horton, Bob Cummings, Gale Gordon, and Doug McClure to name just a few—and of course, with actors like myself who were not as well-known, but working at a craft they loved and making a living at it, which is no small feat. Looking back on those years, I don't remember anyone talking about his or her faith. Not once. I don't mean to imply that they didn't have faith, but if they did, it certainly wasn't discussed.
>
> So, even though I grew up being involved in every activity in my church, I didn't talk about my faith either, and that made it easy to lapse. In those days, I didn't give a person's faith or lack of faith a lot of thought, but in light of how standing up for your faith can affect an actor's career today, I have to wonder if the silence on the subject was purposeful even then.

Fast-forward three decades to the woman I am now—the mother of a severely autistic adult son; and after a thirty-year marriage to the love of my life, a widow for the last fourteen years; the founder of West Virginia's Always Free Honor Flight, honoring hundreds of veterans for the last ten years; president of the Denver Foundation, founded in honor of our son and striving to do what we can to help families dealing with special needs; the author of my memoir, *Gilligan's Dreams*, and of an upcoming children's book, *Four Bears in a Bag*.

The woman I am today is the result of the challenges I faced, something I understood clearly only a few years ago. My son's diagnosis three decades ago set me on a path I didn't even realize I was on. My husband's death forced me to step up, take the reins, and become the woman I believe God intended me to be. Five years ago, while taking a walk, I was thinking back over my life—especially the solo portion of my life—when I had what I call my 'lightning-bolt moment' that literally sent me to my knees in tears. Out of nowhere, I saw God's hand in every facet of my life: the angels He had provided for me for precisely what I needed them for at the exact time I needed them, and the way the events of my life had played out through good and not-so-good choices on my part. He made me hunger to know Him, to read His Word, to understand His grace and mercy. My eyes were opened in a new way to the chaos in the world around me, and my soul knew there had to be more than this brief, earthly existence.

Since that day, I've been studying nonstop, picking the brains of believers who know far more than I. My heart's desire is to glorify God in my daily life, to walk with Him, to know Him as my best friend, to recognize that I am His child and He is my Father and, like my earthly father, He loves me and welcomes me home, regardless of how long I stayed away.

"My cup runneth over" thanks to His grace.

Blessed are the poor in spirit, for theirs is the kingdom of heaven.
—Matthew 5:3

Discussion Questions

1. How does knowing that God speaks to you make a difference in your life?

2. What does this say about who God is?

3. What does this say about how God feels about you?

4. List some of the negatives associated with God "seeing" us.

5. What are some of the positives of God "seeing" us?

6. Why is it important for us to admit to God that we are "worms"?

7. Have you ever admitted to God that you are in spiritual poverty, unable to save yourself, and asked Him to help you?

8. If you have decided to follow Jesus, consider writing down your rags to riches story and sharing it with us online at www.beingthebelieving.com.

To see a video from the author with more thoughts on this topic and to enjoy other resources, please visit www.beingthebelieving.com.

CHAPTER TWO

Good Grief
with Greg McDougal

Blessed are those who mourn, for they shall be comforted.
—Matthew 5:4

The eight Beatitudes should be viewed as stepping stones, with each one building on the next and ultimately culminating in both a powerful position and a blessed state. In the business world, we call this the corporate ladder: you start in an entry-level position, work and claw your way up, and by the time you reach that last rung, you are rewarded with that corner office, a pay raise, position, popularity, and power.

I like to view the Beatitudes as our Lord's version of the corporate ladder, a "Beatitudinal ladder" if you will. We start entry level and work our way up through faith and maturity so that by the time we reach the top, we are well equipped to enjoy the reward found on that last rung.

The first rung of this ladder was found in Matthew 5:3, where Jesus stated, "Blessed are the poor in spirit, for theirs is the kingdom of heaven." Remember, this word "blessed" does not mean happy; happiness is subjective. "Blessed" speaks of an inner satisfaction tethered to salvation in Christ. It is neither subject to emotions nor dependent upon circumstances; it rests in the approval and acceptance of God.

When God blesses us, He is actually approving us. This is a lesson that we all need to learn: to stop seeking approval from others and align ourselves solely with the approval of the Creator. How freeing it is when you stop trying to please everyone around you and simply live for the One within you!

How freeing it is when you stop trying to please everyone around you and simply live for the One within you!

You can exhaust yourself trying to please everyone who comes into your life. Peace only comes when we endeavor to find rest in simply seeking the approval of God.

So, if you are seeking the approval of God, the first step is to acknowledge that you are poor in spirit, or spiritually bankrupt. Admit that salvation is not based on what you do or who you are but on what He has done and who He is.

Salvation is a very personal matter between you and the Lord. It's when you come to a place in your life where you recognize your beggarly-poor state and your need for rescue and come running to the cross to find that there is still room for you there. That is the first rung on this ladder. It must start here.

The reason that so many churches have lost their power is because so many Christians have lost their focus.

Our next Beatitude, found in Matthew 5:4, says, "Blessed are those who mourn, for they shall be comforted."

Renewing Our Focus on Christ

To recognize our sin is to mourn over our condition. The reason that so many churches have lost their power is because so many Christians have lost their focus. And when you take your eyes off Christ, they fall on people. Many "Christians" are causing problems because they are so focused on everyone else. Sadly, some of the most bitter, critical, cynical, unforgiving people you will ever meet sit next to you in church Sunday after Sunday. That is the result of taking your eyes off Christ.

This is the main reason thousands of churches close their doors every single year in our country.[10] Churches are full of people whose focus is off. Oswald J. Smith highlighted this phenomenon when he declared, "The world has become so churchy and the Church so worldly, that it is hard to distinguish the one from the other."[11] Church members might have walked down an aisle, said a prayer, been baptized, and now sing from the choir loft about the power in the blood, but there is no power in their lives because they have never been transformed and regenerated through the gospel of Jesus Christ. In fact, the only evidence many folks offer to be classified as "Christian" are the fish magnets on their cars, Christian music playing on their radios, "Property of God" T-shirts on their backs, or their names on a church membership roll. But there is no change in their lives, no difference.

How do we fix this? By mourning over our sin. By regaining the internal focus required by our Lord. Jesus was an expert at redirecting focus. Remember the story recorded in John 8 of the woman who was caught in adultery? She had a crowd of men lined up and ready to stone her because that crowd had lost its focus. They had overlooked their own sin and set their sights on someone else. Jesus reminded them of the sin in their lives, thereby getting them focused internally once again. That is where we all need to be: internally focused, mourning over our own sin.

To recognize our sin is to mourn over our condition. I was watching a Mark Lowry video the other day[12] in which he stood before a full house and talked about how Jesus started the church with the outcasts of society—the prostitutes, drunkards, fornicators, adulterers, tax collectors, smelly fishermen, and even a Samaritan woman. And the church grew! It grew because one beggar would tell another beggar where the food was. Now that the church has grown, we are inside holding the doors closed, refusing to let anyone else in, because we are judging those outside for sinning differently than we do. It's time we fling those doors open and let them in so that they can experience the peace, position, and power we have found through the gospel of Jesus Christ.

The key to our text: recognizing your own sin and mourning over your own condition.

Lowry then states that he has hated the sin and loved the sinner too long. He said, "I don't have time to hate your sin. Hate your own sin! How about you hate your sin and I'll hate my sin and then we just love on each other?" And there it is, the key to our text: recognizing your own sin and mourning over your own condition.

You might say, "But I don't have sin in my life." I guarantee you do.

> As it is written: "None is righteous, no, not one; no one understands; no one seeks for God. All have turned aside; together they have become worthless; no one does good, not even one."
> **—Romans 3:10–12**

Did you notice that statement, "No one seeks for God"? You did not find God; He was never lost! You are the sinner. You are the one who is lost, and it is God who will find you. When you're bobbing around in life's ocean of trials, in the darkness of your sin, just send up the Matthew

5:3 beacon and confess that you are spiritually bankrupt and in need of rescue.

You must believe in your heart and confess with your mouth that Jesus Christ died and rose again (Romans 10:9) and purposefully and intentionally surrender to His will for your life by repenting of your sins and following Him. And Jesus will pull you right out of those rough waters and set your feet on the dry ground of His love.

Once we are redeemed and rescued, we can't help but love our Father. It has been said that people only know as much about us as we let them know about us. Here is the wonderful truth: God knows everything about us—where we have been, what we have done, what we think, and even what we have yet to do—and He still loves us! Knowing about that kind of love gives us a desire to please Him, so we mourn over our sin.

There was a time that I did not mourn over my sin but celebrated it. During my high school years, we lived in an Airstream trailer next to an orange grove. You can't get more country than that! So, if I were to describe my life before Christ in country lingo, I would say something like this: I was a drinkin', smokin', cussin', fussin', hatin' heathen who was lookin' for love in all the wrong places, hopeless, lost, defeated, and broken in need of a fixin'—but then I heard an old, old story:

How a Savior came from glory, how He gave His life on Calvary to save a wretch like me; I heard about His groaning, of His precious blood's atoning, then I repented of my sins and won the victory.

O victory in Jesus, my Savior, forever. He sought me and bought me with His redeeming blood; He loved me ere I knew Him and all my love is due Him, He plunged me to victory, beneath the cleansing flood.[13]

I know what it took to reconcile this sinner to a holy, almighty God. It took Jesus to don the robes of humanity, endure a mock trial, suffer, bleed, and end His life by hanging on a cruel Roman cross suspended between His home and His creation, being rejected by both. It took God's everything, His only begotten Son. So, knowing what it took to forgive me and set me free, understanding that He knows me better than anyone yet chooses to love me more than everyone, I completely surrender my life to His love. That is why I mourn when I look at my sin, for I am now aware that it hurts the very heart of the only One who has loved me with an everlasting love.

Streams of Tears for the Church

In addition to being concerned enough about our own sin that we actually mourn over it, we are to mourn over the sins of others since we are now aware that their sin hurts the heart of our Father God as well.

> *My eyes shed streams of tears, because people do not keep your law.*
> **—Psalm 119:136**

The words David chose to use speak of utter distress and weakness. In other words, the psalmist is saying that he is crippled and in deep grief—not the kind of crying one does when a toe is stubbed, but the kind of mourning that occurs with the loss of a child. Why is David that upset? Because when someone you love is hurt, you hurt, and our Father hurts when His creation sins. We hear plenty about how sin brings the judgment of God, that God hates sin and punishes the wicked evildoer. But there is another element found in Ephesians 4:29–30: "Let no corrupting talk come out of your mouths, but only such as is good for building up, as fits the occasion, that it may give grace to those who hear. And do not *grieve* the Holy Spirit of God, by whom you were sealed for the day of redemption."

We should mourn over the sins of others because we are motivated by the supernatural love of God to care for others.

First, this text reveals that what grieves the heart of God within the church of God is the disruption of unity caused by the sins of gossip, slander, and contention.

But don't miss what these sins do: they *grieve* the Holy Spirit of God. The Greek word for grieve is *lypeite*, which means to cause grief sorrow, to be "in heaviness."[14] Keeping this in context, according to Ephesians 4:29–30, people who speak against each other or against God are torturing God.

Let me simply ask, in light of what Jesus went through—being rejected, beaten, whipped, forced to carry a cross, and nailed to that same cross on a hill called Mount Calvary, where He suffered, bled, and died—hasn't He been tortured enough? Should we live in such a way as to torture and crucify our Lord again and again? God forbid! So, it should hurt us when Christians sin because we should not want our Lord to suffer anymore.

Not only was Paul willing to postpone heaven, but he was also ready to replace someone in hell. Paul, Jeremiah, and Jesus looked at the sins of humanity and mourned.

We should also mourn over the sins of others because we are motivated by the supernatural love of God to care for others. The Old Testament prophet Jeremiah looked at the sins of humanity and wept so much that he was known as the "weeping prophet."[15]

There are similarities between Jeremiah the weeping prophet and Jesus Christ, as Jesus also wept when He looked at the sins of humanity (Luke 19:41–44). The apostle Paul revealed his care for others when he stated in Philippians 1:23–24, "I am hard pressed between the two. My desire is to depart and be with Christ, for that is far better. But to remain in the flesh is more necessary on your account."

The apostle Paul was willing to postpone heaven for others. Yet even more care for others was evident when he stated in Romans 9:3–4a (NIV), "For I could wish that

I myself were cursed and cut off from Christ for the sake of my people, those of my own race, the people of Israel."

Don't miss that. The apostle Paul cared for others to the degree that not only was he willing to postpone heaven, he was also ready to replace someone in hell. Paul, Jeremiah, and Jesus looked at the sins of humanity and mourned.

The church has become quite proficient in letting this world know what they are against while tragically leaving them wondering what they are for.

When was the last time you really looked at the sins of humanity through the lens of Matthew 5:4 and wept because you cared? To not only know the hurt that your sin brings to God but to see others in sin is to know the separation from God that they face.

Care Enough to Carry the Gospel to the Lost

We've said that the reason so many churches have lost their power is because so many Christians have lost their focus. And what is our focus? It is the Great Commission, to go out into this world and make disciples (Matthew 28:18–20). It is to care enough about the sins of others that we actually exit the doors of the church building, enter the mission field, and boldly proclaim that Jesus Christ has been resurrected and that our Lord lives!

The church has become quite proficient in letting this world know what they are against while tragically leaving them wondering what they are for.

In a recent SBC *Life* magazine article, it was revealed that the number of folks who are making decisions for Christ and following that decision with believer's baptism has not been this low since 1948. Frank Page reminded Southern Baptists of a time when the Convention set a goal ratio of eight to one (8:1). For every eight Southern Baptists, we should see one convert every year, an 8:1 ratio. Now? The ratio of church members to baptisms is more than fifty to one (51:1).[16] This tragically sounds like a joke: How many Baptists does it take to share the gospel and win one for the Kingdom each year? Apparently fifty-one.

Are all your friends saved? Yes? Then make some more friends!

Too many people in the church today have lost focus and are content with where the church is. Speaking to this, Dr. Brian Autry, who serves as Executive Director of the Southern Baptist Conservatives of Virginia, a partnership of more than 750 Southern Baptist churches, proclaimed at a gathering of pastors in Roanoke, "Many have the attitude: 'I'm saved; my wife is saved; our children are saved; and we just don't give a rip about anyone else!'"[17]

When was the last time you presented the gospel to a lost man, woman, boy, or girl? If I were to ask your classmates, coworkers, neighbors, and friends about the last time you told them the story of that old rugged cross, how would they respond?

I am glad you're saved and that your household is all set—I really am. I am excited that you can proclaim that all of your friends and family are saved and that your circle of influence is all accounted for on the train to glory. If that's the case, it's time to move on to another harvest. Are all your friends saved? Yes? Then make some more friends! I am thankful that you have experienced the power and grace of God, that He was able to save you to the uttermost—and if you're any kind of sinner like me, you know that we took a whole lot of saving—but we now have work to do.

We have played around long enough. It's time for us to go out, look around, reach down, open up, and let the gospel go forth.

We are surrounded by a world full of lost people, many of whom do not even see themselves as lost. Yet even more tragic is that with all these folks facing eternal damnation, we do not have enough transformed believers making much of Jesus by bringing these unbelievers the Good News.

We have the light, the hope, the power, the peace, the way, the truth, and the life inside us, yet despite all the folks around us who desperately need to hear the eternal Good News, we are refusing to "make a defense to anyone who asks [us] for a reason for the hope that is in [us]" (1 Peter 3:15).

Oh, we are singing in the choir, teaching Sunday school, and preaching sermons. We are in church every time the doors are open and claim our lives are being changed, yet the harvest is still full of people on their way to eternal separation because we simply do not have laborers for the field.

Mourning over our sin and the sins of others always translates to caring for others. Do we really care about the clerk, the waitress, the mechanic, our nurse or doctor, our exterminator, our neighbors, classmates, family, friends, and coworkers?

We have played around long enough. It's time for us to go out, look around, reach down, open up, and let the gospel go forth.

Getting to a place where we mourn over our sin and the sins of those around us can make us very uncomfortable, yet only through mourning can we hope to receive comfort. "Blessed are those who mourn, for they shall be comforted" (Matthew 5:4).

Chuck Colson, in his book *Who Speaks for God?*, writes, "In sin we carry around baggage, scars, fear, guilt, shame and doubt. Yet Jesus Christ tells us all today that when we mourn over that very sin, He will give comfort. He is telling you today to look to yourself, acknowledge your sin, mourn over it, and immediately you will see your baggage dropped, scars healed, fear replaced with trust, shame changed to boldness and doubt converted to faith."[18]

Aren't you tired? Isn't life hard enough without the internal struggles? Don't you long for a safe place to fall? Don't you long for a time when you are so overwhelmed with acceptance, approval, power, joy, and love that you can leave your tears in the valley and dance on the mountaintop?

Mourn over your sin. This is the paradox of the Beatitudes, truth flipped on its head. If you want comfort, you must mourn. You must be willing to become concerned over the sin in your own life, understanding that it is hurting the heart of the One who gave you life, and you must be willing to become painfully aware that the sins of others affect the heart of God as well.

From Grief to Agreement

If you want to be blessed by God, you must weep over your sins and the sins of those around you, knowing that as you cry out, you will receive the comfort that only God can give as the Great Physician.

You see, grief can be good. And there is no story that exemplifies this thought better than this story from another friend of mine, Greg McDougal. Greg was named Music Evangelist of the Year in the 2010, Inspirational Country Music Awards and Musician of the Year in the 2012 awards.[19] He and I both graduated from Pasco High School in 1987, but we lost touch and didn't reconnect until a few years ago. Greg has a story to tell, birthed from a life that proclaims, "Good grief!" Here is some of that story in his own words:

Growing up, I went to church. My grandpa was a preacher. My uncle was a preacher. Seems my whole family sang country/gospel music for as long as I can remember. It also seems like there was never a time that I didn't know about Jesus Christ, the cross, and that He died for my sins. I knew how to dress, I knew how to bow my head to pray, I knew how to stand and sing "I'll Fly Away." I also knew how to sit still in the pew so that my momma didn't reach up and help me! A hymnal can bring about a real attitude adjustment when physically applied.

While I was growing up, one of the enemy's biggest tricks at our house was to get us to treat faith as if it were a Sunday morning thing only. Oh, and a prayer right before we ate. As I tell you of how my dad had failed in leading our family in faith, I say it with all humility and an understanding of just how easy it can be to fail so miserably myself. After my parents divorced, we stopped going to church, and gradually, my musical direction turned from gospel to secular. "A little leaven leavens the whole lump" (Galatians 5:9 NKJV).

At some point, I said, "Lord, if it's all the same to you, I'll take my inheritance and spend it the way I want to." Looking back at those years as a prodigal son, I can see that God was at work and using those old gospel songs in my life to get me to touch "home plate" from time to time. I met my wife, Diane, in Florida. We got married and right away moved to Nashville, Tennessee. Next thing you know, Atlantic recording artist John Michael Montgomery recorded a song that I had cowritten. I then got hired to play acoustic guitar and sing backup for Epic recording artist Stephanie Bentley. At the height of my time on Music Row, I signed another publishing deal with EMI Music with the plan to make a record and pitch it for a recording contract on a major label.

"There is a way that seems right to a man, but its end is the way of death" (Proverbs 14:12 NKJV).

How many prodigals do you know? Amazing that one common denominator is that we all spend our inheritance on foolishness and treachery. I met a few professionals in the music business who purposed and succeeded at being salt and light and a steadfast witness for Christ.

Unfortunately, I failed. Or rather, that was not my stated purpose. Climbing on a tour bus equated to party time. The applause and accolades were my drug of choice, which all too often led to self-indulgences of other kinds.

"...for they loved the praise of men more than the praise of God" (John 12:43 NKJV).

You see, another common denominator amongst us prodigals is the notion—conscious or not—that this is all about me. From childhood, it was easy to be doted on and fussed about. All I had to do was grab my guitar, sing a song—gospel or not—and work to be the best I could be so that I could get that next rush of approval.

And yet, He fearfully and wonderfully made you and me and gave us gifts. He caused a guitar to be put in my hand at seven years old as a vehicle for me to use my voice to worship. So many times, I've stood in front of a group of people to sing. Along with my twin brother and two sisters, I sang over and over again, "And I thank God for the Lighthouse, I owe my life to Him...." I'm the one who did not know for the longest time that He had given me that ability and it was to be used for Him. I'm the one who took the detour.

"In all your ways acknowledge Him, and He shall direct your path" (Proverbs 3:6 NKJV).

As I take the score and review the math, every one of my failures stems from leaning on my own understanding. From not being prepared with God's Word so that I can agree with Him.

For a long time, I just didn't understand how much it meant to simply agree with God. That is, until I'd had enough of the results of not agreeing with God.

He knows I need a Savior. He says we all need a Savior. "For by grace you have been saved through faith; and that not of yourselves, it is the gift of God, not of works, lest anyone should boast" (Ephesians 2:8–9 NKJV).

If you are reading this and you have been walking in shame and condemnation, if you are of the opinion that you have sinned far greater than what He will forgive, you are wrong. "If we confess our sins, He is faithful and just to forgive us our sins and to cleanse us from all unrighteousness" (1 John 1:9 NKJV).

In 1996, we were still in the music business, but God made sure my wife and I moved in next door to some crazy people who would not leave us alone about going to church with them. We finally went to Sunday School class with them just to shut them up and get them off our backs. We began hearing the Word of God.

After, we both agreed with God about His free gift of forgiveness through Jesus Christ. "That if you confess with your mouth the Lord Jesus and believe in your heart that God has raised Him from the dead, you will be saved" (Romans 10:9 NKJV).

We prayed together for the first time and said, "Okay, Lord, whatever it is you may have for us to do, that is what we'll do." We had been trying to have children for a while with no results, but the very next week we found out that we would be having our first child. Nine months later, Jeffrey was born, and he was beautiful. We cried so hard from the immeasurable joy. But as more doctors and nurses came in and our son was rushed out of the room, we literally did not know if we would ever see him alive again. We cried uncontrollably from the fear. We thought we were all alone in that little delivery room for just a minute or two. But then someone put a phone call into that church that our neighbors bugged us to no end to go to. What happened next is what we have spent the last thirteen years going and telling about. That day when we saw exactly what Jesus meant when He said, "By this all will know that you are My disciples, if you have love for one another" (John 13:35 NKJV).

We wound up having four beautiful children. Three of the four wound up being diagnosed with cystic fibrosis. They spent their childhood on the road, standing up and singing as The McDougal Kids: "And I thank God for the Lighthouse, I owe my life to Him" As I write this, we are still reeling from losing our nineteen-year-old son Sean in January 2019.

But as I write this, I *know* that I know that God indeed redeems all things through Christ. That He indeed takes what the enemy meant for evil and makes for good (Genesis 50:20). That He means it when He says, "Fear not. For you have been redeemed. I have called you by name. You are Mine! You know not the thoughts I think towards you.

Thoughts of peace and not of evil. To bring you to an expected end" (Isaiah 43:1 and Jeremiah 29:11, paraphrases). He has shown us in so many ways of His trustworthiness and His faithfulness.

Heaven is more real to us than ever before. Because of God's promises through His Word, we know that our son is healed and whole and now in a perfect body. The questions we might have about why and why not, well, God had been busy teaching us to trust Him while Sean was with us. The only peace we find is to simply agree with the grace, mercy, and sovereignty of our heavenly Father. "And the Lord said, 'Simon, Simon! Indeed, Satan has asked for you, that he may sift you as wheat. But I have prayed for you, that your faith should not fail; and when you have returned to Me, strengthen your brethren'" (Luke 22:31–34 NKJV).

Rev. Greg McDougal

President, The Work of a Carpenter Ministries, Inc.

www.theworkofacarpenterministries.org

Blessed are they that mourn: for they shall be comforted.
—Matthew 5:4

Discussion Questions

1. When was the last time you wept real tears over the sin in your life?

2. What took place between you and God when you cried out to Him over your sin?

3. When you see someone else in sin, what is your response? Why?

4. Why do you think it is easy to judge others for sinning differently than you do?

5. What kind of comfort does Jesus provide to those who cry out over their sin?

6. Is there a sin in your life that you are not crying over and confessing because you like it too much?

7. What do you think would happen if you finally decided to mourn over *all* of your sin?

To see a video from the author with more thoughts on this topic and to enjoy more resources, please visit www.beingthebelieving.com.

CHAPTER THREE

Gentle Giants
with Sam Sorbo

Blessed are the meek, for they shall inherit the earth.
—Matthew 5:5

There are eight Beatitudes found in Matthew 5. They define and describe the responsibilities and expectations of the Christian and reveal the rewards for such a life.

Scholars have divided the eight Beatitudes into two sections. The first four deal with our relationship with God, and the last four focus on the relationships we have with one another.

If we have learned anything from Old Testament law, it is that we lack both the capacity to fulfill it and the desire to do so. This is the beauty of Christianity: all that God requires of us, He provides us, which includes both the capacity to fulfill and the desire to complete the law.

Culture after culture has tried to legislate morality. In other words, blanket humanity with legislation, financially back the enforcement of those laws, and then hope for the best.

This has always failed, and it always will. Why? We simply lack the capacity and desire to do good. Remember Romans 3:11: "None is righteous, no, not one; no one understands; no one seeks for God." All have turned aside; together they have become worthless; no one does good, not even one."

Before God lays out the expectations He has in living for Him, He reveals that the capacity and desire to do so come from Him.

There are two beautiful lessons to be learned in the division of the Beatitudes. As stated previously, the first four deal with our vertical relationship with God and the last four deal with our horizontal relationship to others. Basically, before God lays out the expectations He has in living *for* Him, He reveals that the capacity and desire to do so come *from* Him.

Secondly, in this division of the Beatitudes we find something else amazing that Christ has done. Though initially God issued ten commandments for believers to follow in the Old Testament, some Jewish scholars and rabbis have added to them over the millennia. According to Jewish tradition, there are 613 commandments in the Torah, which are the first five books of the Old Testament.[20]

Don't miss what Jesus Christ has done and the freeing beauty found in the religion of Christianity. During the earthly ministry of Jesus Christ, someone stepped up and asked Him:

> *"Teacher, which is the greatest commandment in the Law?" And he said to him, "You shall love the Lord your God with all your heart and with all your soul and with all your mind. This is the great and first commandment. And a second is like it: You shall love your neighbor as yourself. On these two commandments depend all the Law and the Prophets."*
>
> **—Matthew 22:36–40**

To start a relationship with God, you must come to a place in your life where you need a relationship with God.

Did you get that? Jesus looked at Judaism, with its hundreds of complicated laws, and essentially said, "Love God and love each other, and I will give you the capacity and desire to do both!"

So, our first rung on the Beatitudinal ladder, our first step in our relationship to God, was found in Matthew 5:3: "Blessed are the poor in spirit, for theirs is the kingdom of heaven." To start a relationship with God, you must come to a place in your life where you *need* a relationship with God.

The second step in our relationship with God is found in Matthew 5:4, which says, "Blessed are those who mourn, for they shall be comforted." Once we discover that God loves us and we surrender to that love by loving Him back, we hurt when He hurts. And what hurts Him the most is when His creation sins against Him. We mourn over our sins and the sins of others because those sins hurt the very heart of the only One who has loved us with an everlasting love.

Now we come to the third of four steps in our relationship with God, found in Matthew 5:5, which says, "Blessed are the meek, for they shall inherit the earth."

Let me define meekness by first stating what it is not. Meekness is not:

A Lack of Confidence, or Being Wishy-Washy

Meekness is not describing someone who is shy, withdrawn, or introverted; someone who lacks confidence or is wishy-washy; or someone who goes along with the flow of culture. Paul tells us that "God gave us a spirit not of fear but of power and love and self-control" (2 Timothy 1:7). If anyone should be walking around with confidence and boldness, exhibiting power in their lives and demonstrating conviction, it should be a child of the King!

I stand convinced that one of the reasons for the current state of moral decay in America is that many Christians and churches have intentionally benched themselves out of fear of scorn from unbelievers. Timidity about the things of God and wishy-washiness about biblical truth, as we rationalize that God will somehow honor us for our meekness toward the sin in the world, has led to more scorn, not more glory, for the name of Christ.

Meekness does not speak of someone who lacks confidence or convictions, or who is wishy-washy. Neither does it speak of:

Weakness

Meekness is not speaking of someone who is a doormat to those around them. Christians fall into two groups when they allow others to dominate, control, manipulate, or use them. In the first group, we find those who are motivated extrinsically. In other words, they have been told for so long by so many that they are worthless, no good, and inferior that they now believe within themselves that they have no voice and no value. Many people would have Christians believe that they are powerless, but remember: "God gave us a spirit not of fear but of power and love and self-control" (2 Timothy 1:7).

The second group is motivated intrinsically. These people have a desire to be pushed around by others because they think meekness means weakness and that by being weak for God, they stand to be rewarded. These folks represent a kind of masochistic Christian martyr, in that they believe, by their sacrificial display of weakness, they stand to be rewarded by God through blessings.

Paul says in Philippians 4:13, "I can do all things through him who strengthens me." We are not weak, because Christ Himself supplies our strength!

So, if meekness does not mean weakness or a lack of confidence, what does it mean? The Greek word for "meek" is *praus*, and in our text is a picture-word that was used for at least three things: a gentle breeze, a soothing medicine, and a tamed wild animal.[21]

A gentle breeze. An unstoppable yet gentle breeze that caresses as it affects change. While not seen directly, its effects are evident from leaves moving, seeds spreading, ships given power, and a tired bird given a much-needed boost. May we endeavor to be a gentle breeze in this spiritually dry and parched world, a breeze that soothes, cools, invigorates, and refreshes the lives of those around us.

Soothing medicine. This speaks of a remedy that does not taste bad or cause other issues and side effects. It heals without creating additional pain. In contrast to the days when medicine consisted of a leather belt to bite down on and a shot of whiskey to mask the pain, meekness speaks of a soothing medicine that heals, gently caressing and affecting change.

In 2 Chronicles 7:14, after King Solomon had dedicated the temple of the Lord, God appeared to him in the night and said:

> *If my people who are called by my name humble themselves, and pray and seek my face and turn from their wicked ways, then I will hear from heaven and will forgive their sin and heal their land.*

This world is sick and in need of healing. The sickness is sin, and the medicine is the gospel of Jesus Christ. And while we are to take that medicine to the sick, we are not to try to force it aggressively down their throats so that they push it away. It's simple Mary Poppins practicality: "A spoonful of sugar helps the medicine go down!"[22] Remember that person who first shared Jesus with you? I would bet that they didn't thump you on the head with the biggest King James Bible sold, shouting that unless you repented, you would burn for all eternity in a place called hell! If I were a betting man, I would say that someone cared enough *about you* to build a relationship *with you* and they communicated in love the message of the cross *to you,* like a soothing medicine.

A tamed wild animal. Lastly, and more accurately, this word *meek* in the original Greek language relates to an animal, such as a horse, that's tamed, or trained to be gentle.[23] That is precisely what Jesus means when He says that we are to be meek. We are to be full of potential and power, yet subdued and in control.

God has given us His power, and He has also given us the power to control that power.

So, the best definition I have ever heard for meekness? Power under control.

God has given us His power, and He has also given us the power to control that power. What power?

- The "gesture of a finger" power of God that was used in creation (see Isaiah 40:12) and the "moving hand of God" power used to destroy creation (see 1 Chronicles 21:15).

- The "parting of the waters" power that brought deliverance through Moses to the Jewish people living in Egypt (see Exodus 14:21) and the "closing in of the waters" power that brought destruction to the Egyptians pursuing them as they escaped (see Exodus 14:28).

- The "resurrection of the dead" power (John 11:43). The "sealing up the heavens" power and the "opening up of the heavens" power (see 1 Kings 8:35). The "causing of the blind to see, the deaf to hear, the dumb to talk, and the lame to walk" power (see Matthew 11:5).

- The "taking a bottle out of the hand and putting a Bible in it" power. The "taking a mouth of blasphemy and replacing it with a mouth of praise" power. And the "transforming the reproach in the community to a blessing in the community" power.

That power is in us! So, the question is, what do we *do* with that power? As the old adage says, with great power comes an equal measure of responsibility.

The Responsibility in Meekness—What It Does

So, now that we have established that meekness is power under control, how do we employ it in our lives? Simply put, we are to be Gentle Giants. There are times in this life when we must be gentle, and there are times when we must be giantlike.

There are times we must be quiet, step down, be subdued and reserved, like a sweet old granny deferring to what her grandchildren would like to do when they come over for a visit. We must be, in a word, gentle.

Then there are times that we must be vocal and step up, be proactive, like a seasoned warrior on the battleground, with a sword in one hand and the Bible in the other. We must be giantlike, unafraid to rise up and take a stand for what we believe in.

The question is: When are we to be gentle, and when are we to be giantlike?

Be Gentle Regarding Your Feelings, Emotions, Pride, and Preferences

The founder of our faith, Jesus Christ, set the bar high, but He did not leave us in the dark as to what to do because He was willing to demonstrate His expectations through His life. First Peter 2:21–23 reveals that "Christ also suffered for you, leaving you an example, so that you might follow in his steps. He committed no sin, neither was deceit found in his mouth. When he was reviled, he did not revile in return; when he suffered, he did not threaten, but continued entrusting himself to him who judges justly."

With Jesus Christ as our standard and example, we should be ashamed when we get all riled up when someone sits in our seat, the preacher doesn't shake our hand, someone cuts us off in traffic, our boss dumps a pile of work on our desk at 4:45 p.m. on a Friday, or the church doesn't go where we want on a mission trip. When it comes to your preferences, vision, dreams, and goals, be gentle. Even secular psychiatrists, like Dr. Phil, often challenge couples in conflict with the question, "Do you want to be right or happy?"[24] As Christians, indwelled with supernatural power, we should be proactive in our efforts to sacrifice our right to be right on the altar of unity.

We should be proactive in our efforts to sacrifice our right to be right on the altar of unity.

A few years ago, a local congregation became the center of attention as division and conflict marked what was once a thriving and growing church. Ultimately, more than fifty households abandoned their spiritual home, and the effects on the church persisted for decades afterward. What possibly could have caused such a rift? A shift in doctrine? The moral failure of the pastor?

No. It was the position of the pulpit in the sanctuary. Now, don't be quick to discount this as an isolated incident. Many congregations have been divided over such trivial issues: the color of the carpet, song preference, Bible translations, and even the length of the minister's sermon.

We must remember that the world is watching. If this world simply sees another organization whose members are struggling to get along and love one another, they will walk away unchanged, and that can prove eternally damning, something none of us should hope to give an account for. Sacrificing your right to be right, being gentle, means that you will not have to stand before God to give an account of why you were the reason someone didn't come to church, or worse, why they rejected Christ.

Be a Giant Against Sin and Falsehood

I received my driver's license while living in a rural town in Florida with my grandparents. At that time, my grandfather offered me his Grand Marquis to practice with. According to him, the engine was huge and full of power. The maximum speed for any road in our county was forty-five miles per hour, which frustrated me, as I wanted to feel the "power" of which Pop-Pop spoke. I will never forget asking Pop-Pop when I could put that pedal to the metal and see what that engine could do. He replied, "Tom, only after you have proven you can handle these back roads and the slow speeds will we go on the highway and let you use that power." What a great analogy for the Christian faith and the power that God has given us!

So, after practicing on the back roads of life with slow speeds—that is, keeping our God-given power under wraps and sacrificing our preferences—when can we really let the power out and be giants? Be a giant when it comes to how others are treated and the truth. As recorded in Matthew 21:12, when Jesus went to the temple and found it had been turned from a house of prayer into a den of thieves, He flipped the tables and drove out all the moneychangers! And yet, He did not sin in any of that. Likewise, we are told that it is okay to be angry. We are just not to sin in that anger (Ephesians 4:26).

When do I, Tom McCracken, get angry and become a giant? When people proclaim that Jesus Christ is not the Son of God, that He was not born of a virgin, or that He did not physically rise from the grave and defeat death. I become angry when scholars and scientists insist that the Bible is simply outdated gibberish written by a bunch of uneducated Bedouin tribesman, or that there is no such thing as a literal heaven or hell, or that my Jesus did not die for everyone. That's when I become a giant!

Let me witness division in God's house, conflict between brothers and sisters in Christ, and I will show you what a modern-day Goliath looks like!

When I see a child who is abused, a woman who is hurt, a person with a disability who is mocked, a senior citizen who is taken advantage of, or a student who is bullied, my giant comes out. If you mess with me, I should be gentle. But if you mess with other people or with doctrine and truth, I become a giant.

A few years ago, one of our church members, an eighty-five-year-old woman, was at home in bed sleeping when someone leaned a ladder against her upstairs window, broke in, dragged her out of bed, threw her to the ground, beat her, raped her, and left her for dead. All I will say is that my church family and community saw the giant in me come out.

But you don't need to be all *giant* all the time or all *gentle* all the time. God is not calling for that in our lives. It is all about balance, about using our God-given power to control our God-given power.

Years ago, I was called to pastor an established church that was committee-run, an environment where the pastor was treated not as a God-called leader but as an employee to be directed and evaluated by the personnel committee and deacons.

The first three years were relatively quiet until some of my decisions were challenged and lines were drawn, at which point my entire family was relentlessly attacked by a few key carnal people in leadership.

Toward the end of my five-year tenure, my three girls—ages four, seven, and eight—unbeknownst to me, had been passed over during Communion, had parts in the Christmas play taken away from them, and were kicked out of the children's choir.

My son, who was eighteen at the time, had church members call his work and school, spreading vicious and reputation-altering lies about him. It was so bad that he had to leave his career and college and join the Army just to escape.

After nine years in the Army with two tours in Afghanistan and one in Iraq, he was honorably discharged. He suffers from PTSD and to date wants nothing to do with Christ or His church.

The fact is, even if you have a good plan for your life, God's plan is better because He knows more than you!

I endeavored to be a gentle giant while I addressed these issues, following the Lord's leading as to how I should respond. I had every reason to go into giant mode and take a stand against these church members who had hurt my family, but God guided me to gently resign my position and remove my family from that environment. He then directed me to start a church that was focused on unity. Had I decided to ignore God's leading and be a giant instead of being gentle, to use that strength and power instead of controlling it, CommUNITY Church would never have been born.

The Resources for Meekness—How It Is Done

So now you know *what* meekness is, *why* it's important, and *when* it is to be used. The question remains, *how* can we be meek? We all know how hard it is to love when hated, pray when persecuted, and turn the other cheek when struck.

The key is found in Psalm 37, which is what Jesus was referring to with this specific Beatitude. So, to understand how to be meek, we must understand the reference to Psalm 37.

> *Commit your way to the LORD; trust in him, and he will act. He will bring forth your righteousness as the light, and your justice as the noonday. Be still before the LORD and wait patiently for him; fret not yourself over the one who prospers in his way, over the man who carries out evil devices!*
>
> **—Psalm 37:5–7**

There are four ideals in this text that, if evident in our lives, will result in meekness:

Trust in God (v. 5b)
"Trust in him, and he will act."

If you are to be a Gentle Giant, using the power to control the power, you must learn to trust God completely. Understand that life will be hard, won't make sense, and at times, can't be explained.

You must come to the place where you acknowledge that His ways are not your ways and His thoughts are not your thoughts (Isaiah 55:8–9). You get to a place of spiritual maturity where you stop trying to figure out the mind of God and simply trust the heart of God. You stop trying to figure out why God does what He does and simply trust that your Father knows what is best for your life. The fact is, even if you have a good plan for your life, God's plan is better because He knows more than you!

Trust God so completely that no matter what is going on in your life, He is sufficient, satisfying, and enough for you. As John Piper says, "God is most glorified in us when we are most satisfied in Him."[25] It is all about making Romans 8:28 your life verse: "…we know that for those who love God all things work together for good, for those who are called according to his purpose."

You see, people who trust *in* God are those who recognize that nothing will come *into* their life that hasn't first been filtered through the loving will of God *for* their life. Trust in God means believing that nothing catches Him off guard or by surprise. Trust in God means believing that no circumstance in your life will find God pacing the halls of glory, wringing His hands and wondering what to do next.

Commit to God (v. 5a)
"Commit your way to the LORD"

Gol, the Hebrew word for "commit" here, means "to roll," which has two implications.[26]

First, it speaks of something precious being rolled up in a protective layer. This word conjures up the image of a precious and valuable gem being rolled up in a piece of velvet and placed in the security of a safe. Likewise, since we are precious and valuable in the eyes of God, we are rolled up in His Son Jesus Christ and placed in the security of His right hand (John 10:28).

Paul puts it this way: "…whether Paul or Apollos or Cephas or the world or life or death or the present or the future—all are yours, and you are Christ's, and Christ is God's" (1 Corinthians 3:22).

This word can also speak of a stone that is rolling down a hill. While there may be small obstacles in the way of the stone, because of the steep slope, the stone eventually makes it to the bottom. We too can roll like a stone down the hills of this world. Because we are in Christ, we don't have to let this world get us down. We can roll with it, knowing that whatever obstacles we encounter, all things will work out through our love for Him. Yes, this journey is hard, with plenty of obstacles along the way, but as long as we are moving in His direction, we have assurance that everything will eventually work out for our good.

You are rolled up in God so that you can roll in this world, making progress, passing by and through obstacles, and not stopping long enough to get caught up in a mess. Paul knew this truth, and that is why he reminded us to "press on toward the goal for the prize of the upward call of God in Christ Jesus" (Philippians 3:14).

Quiet Before God (v. 7a)
"Be still before the LORD and wait patiently for him"

If you are like me, patience is not your strong point! At best, we are like that guy who went to the top of the mountain and prayed to God, "Lord, give me patience and give it to me now!"

In our busy and instantaneous culture, patience and rest are needed more than ever. Our society is characterized by restlessness. Gone are the days of loyalty, commitment, dedication, and perseverance. Now we find it common and "normal" to jump from job to job, relationship to relationship, and church to church. By waiting on the Lord and having patience, you will see a reward that would not have been realized if you had bailed out and moved on too soon.

Another issue is that, to satisfy this restlessness inherent in our culture, we fill our schedules. If you are not careful, you will fill your schedule to the point that when you finally lay down for the night, you will realize that you didn't take any time during the day to be still and know that God is God.

You might be thinking, "But I talk to God plenty. I bring Him all of my worries, troubles, fears, requests, petitions, and prayers."

I am sure you do. But honestly, when was the last time you went into a prayer closet, turned off your phone, got quiet, and just listened to Him speak to you for more than a few minutes?

I remember a project I was given when attending seminary at Liberty University. My professor asked us to turn off our phones and go into a closet, without a watch, and pray for thirty minutes. Well, I was rather presumptuous and cocky. From the outset, I knew that as a pastor, I would impress this guy with a paper that boasted at least an hour of prayer. Thirty minutes sounded so superficial. I mean, my sermons are justifiably forty-five minutes long, because you can't communicate anything of importance in less time than that.

While it's great that we take time to speak to God, it is even better to take the time to listen to God speak to us.

So, into the closet I went. I started praying for my family, then moved on to my church family, then my neighborhood, the missionaries we support, the sick and afflicted, and then I gave time to be still and listen to what He wanted to say to me. After what I thought was at least an hour, I exited the closet, grabbed my watch, and looked at it with pride. To my great shock, I discovered that I had been in that closet in prayer for just twenty minutes! We are just not used to being still and displaying patience.

What I have learned in the years since that project is that while it's great that we take time to speak to God, it is even better to take the time to listen to God speak to us.

Do Not Fret for God (v. 7b)
"Fret not yourself over the one who prospers in his way, over the man who carries out evil devices."

Humanity has always struggled with the reality that evil people often prosper while godly people suffer. That is why God has lifted the burden of this question from His children's shoulders. You see, we don't have to figure out who did wrong and what their judgment should be. That is God's responsibility, not ours.

While we only see what people do, God sees why they do what they do, and that makes Him the only One qualified to serve as Judge.

The message from Paul is: "Beloved, never avenge yourselves, but leave it to the wrath of God, for it is written, 'Vengeance is mine, I will repay, says the Lord'" (Romans 12:19). I know this may be offensive to you, but as much as you like helping God take care of business, God does not need your help! While we only see *what* people do, God sees *why* they do what they do, and that makes Him the only One qualified to serve as Judge.

So, to be meek you must trust and commit to God, be still before God, and fret not on God's behalf.

The Rewards for Meekness—What it Gives
"Blessed are the meek, for they shall inherit the earth."
(Matthew 5:5)

What is the reward for being meek? We inherit the earth! I don't know about you, but I am looking at this reward and wondering, "Really? What I get for being meek is to inherit the earth?" Have you looked at this place lately? I mean, maybe it was great before Adam and Eve ate from the tree and messed everything up. But now, there are thorns on the roses, dust in the air, animals wanting to eat humans, war, pestilence, sickness, disease, and terrorism. And don't even get me started on the earthquakes, typhoons, hurricanes, tornadoes, and blizzards. Or that my favorite dessert, a chocolate volcano cake, has two thousand calories! So why does Jesus make inheriting the earth sound like such a reward? Well, actually, the reward is twofold:

Rewards Now

To inherit the earth means we can have confidence that there is coming a day when Jesus Christ will fix everything broken and make all wrongs right. We can have confidence, as we look around and see the sinner celebrating in prosperity with the bigger house, the better job, and the nicer car, that it all belongs to our Father and our Father has given it all to us. Maybe not now, but I assure you, it will be worth the wait.

Trust me, you'll get down and discouraged, and this world will say you are justified in that. And I could join you on that path. I have an incurable kidney disease, high blood pressure, diverticulosis, high cholesterol, two herniated discs that require procedures every six months, two shoulders that have endured five major surgeries, severe repressed migraine syndrome as a result of a moderate traumatic brain injury from a military accident, not to mention the cyst in my foot, tinnitus, two hernias, and now possibly ulcers! Oh, I could get discouraged, but I choose to claim the peace, joy, and power that come from the confidence I have that one day soon, either through the casket or the clouds, I will be in the presence of my King and there proclaim that it has been worth it all!

I heard the story of a janitor who worked at a seminary. One day he was sitting outside during his lunch break, reading the Bible. A theology professor who was walking to his next class noticed this janitor reading from the book of Revelation and asked, in a rather snobby tone, "Do you actually *understand* the meaning of what you are reading?" To which the janitor replied, "Yes sir, Jesus is gonna win!" That is the gift of this text, the reason Jesus calls this a reward, for we find a confidence and assurance that comes from God in knowing how it all ends; a confidence and assurance, through faith, that rewards us now.

Rewards Later

We can have confidence in the blessed hope. We can have faith. But there is coming a day when we will be able to trade our faith in for sight at the gates of glory. We will walk through those gates of pearl, dance on the streets of gold, touch the walls of jasper, and jump up and down on a foundation of precious stone, enjoying that place of big doors and no mores while meeting the greats and the saints, as we make our way up to that mansion on the hilltop to claim our inheritance through Christ Jesus to worship our Father forever and ever. I may not be a prosperity preacher down here, but I assure you, I will be one up there!

And, let me say that for me, the future reward I am most looking forward to up there, that gives me hope and joy down here, is not what is in heaven as much as what is not.

According to Revelation 21:4, there will be no more:

- *Trials.* No more disease, sickness, aches, and pains. In fact, there is coming a day when God will put every hospital, nursing home, and funeral home out of business!

- *Tears.* No more weeping over a wayward child, an unsaved spouse, or the loss of a loved one. No more sleepless nights crying into the pillow, feeling misunderstood and unloved. One day God Himself will wipe every tear from our eyes.

- *Temptations.* For me, this is what I look forward to most about heaven, that not only will my worship be without deterioration, distraction and disruption; all of which tempt me to take my eyes off of Jesus, but that I will never again be in a position of yielding to temptation and hurting my Father's heart.

The meek inherit the earth—no wonder John was pleading for Christ to return soon when, from a rocky island of isolation, after being banished by the government, he cried out, "Amen. Come, Lord Jesus!" (Revelation 22:20b). John was a gentle giant that knew the reward that awaited him. Are you?

For this beatitude, I reached out to a new friend of mine, Sam Sorbo. My wife and I had the honor of breaking bread with Sam during a banquet for the Happy Trails

Convention in Roanoke, put on by our mutual friends, Dr. Fredric and Carol Eichelman. Being in the entertainment industry, Sam has seen her share of pride and vanity, yet has navigated that world with dignity, class and humility. Here is what she says about meekness:

> This may be the most overlooked or ignored of the beatitudes.
>
> Why? Because today we equate the word meek with weak and we know that weakness does not prevail. Not in this world. A creature who is meek, by current definition standards, is an individual devoid of courage and self-respect, of no use to himself or anyone else. Perhaps he is a hypocrite: fearful, impotent at the very least, ineffective, and useless.
>
> But our common definition of meek today is not the same as the word Jesus chose for His message in His Sermon on the Mount, however. There is no single word for this concept in our language today. The true significance of the word meek, as used in the Bible, is power, under control.

Power, Under Control

> It is tragic that the meaning of the words that Jesus used are so distorted today. Worse, our revised interpretation encourages the exact opposite of what Jesus intended! This misunderstanding, promoted in our culture, certainly makes His words and His commission easier to reject.
>
> Isn't that suspicious?
>
> Moses stood up to the most powerful man in the world Pharaoh Ramses—a god in his own mind—and led an entire country out of bondage. Numbers

12:3 says, "Now the man Moses was very meek, more than all people who were on the face of the earth." Moses' meekness placed him above all other men? That cannot refer to a quality of weakness, certainly.

Jesus confronted and calmed the winds and the waves (Matthew 8:23–27). He chased the money-changers out of the temple (Matthew 21:12–17) and criticized the Pharisees—the most powerful political body in the region, next to the Roman government—but in Matthew 11:29, He says Himself, "Take my yolk upon you, and learn of me; for I am meek and lowly in heart: and ye shall find rest unto your souls" (KJV).

He said, "I am meek," and yet He did the strongest thing, voluntarily. "Greater love has no one than this, that someone lay down his life for his friends." He did that, and so, would this act be considered meek by our current understanding of the word? He spoke of His meekness giving our souls rest. Giving someone else a rest implies a provision of potent strength, not withering weakness.

So, let's examine power under control, the definition of meekness as close as we can come. What is its source? For our Biblical heroes, it meant righteousness. It's not the out-of-control power on the streets of New York, or Portland, where mercenary protestors foment rage amongst a misinformed and easily manipulated public. It's not a disengagement from the truth. Righteous means morally good, following religious or moral laws.

Being meek does not mean to shrink from a fight. It means to bring righteous power and moral conviction to the fight. It means to engage, like Moses did, despite his fearfulness, with Pharaoh. Remember how Moses argued with God when he was chosen (Exodus 3: 11, 13)? He first said he couldn't represent the people of Israel because they wouldn't recognize that God had sent him, so God turned his staff into a serpent and then back again (Exodus 4:1–5). Then God smote Moses' hand with leprosy and healed it again for him (Exodus 4:6–7). Even after this, Moses continued to protest, saying, "O Lord, I'm not very good with words. I never have been, and I'm not now, even though you have spoken to me. I get tongue-tied, and my words get tangled" (Exodus 4:10 NLT). In these verses, we see the current definition of meekness played out, but it isn't fair to leave the story half-unread, because this isn't the portion that earned him the accolade of meek!

Moses continued to argue with God until God's anger was kindled and He sought a solution to the stubborn, disobedient Moses. He proposed Moses' brother, Aaron, who did not stutter (Exodus 4:14–17). A "meek" person today (by our current definition) would never argue with God as Moses did. More importantly, a weak person today would never seek an audience with Pharaoh, much less demand anything of him – certainly not the release of 2.4 million slaves. In fact, God told Moses that Pharaoh's heart would be hardened and he would refuse Moses' request, despite the incredible power that Moses would display to the Egyptian leader (Exodus 3:19).

Power, under control.

Jesus overturned the money-changers' tables on the temple steps (Matthew 21:12–17). He antagonized the political powers by performing miracles on the Sabbath. He never went in search of a fight, but the evildoers unabashedly brought the fight to Him, and tried to trap Him several times. Jesus gave us the perfect role model for bracing ourselves against an ethos of iniquity. Our culture seeks to intimidate Christians into silence, but Jesus' example shows us that silence is not our only course of action, and results indicate beyond doubt that silence and weakness usher in the loss of our moral values and Judeo-Christian culture. Reluctant though we may be, if we endeavor to follow Jesus, we ought to take his words to heart. He was powerful for the truth, while remaining controlled in His actions.

We need more of these kinds of heroes today: standing firm in the truth, as Moses and Jesus did, against the prevailing pernicious political forces. Don't believe Christians should not be involved in politics, when two of our most prominent biblical role-models purposely made politics the linchpins of their ministries. Although our current definition of meekness might imply that Jesus wanted to discourage us from the fight, the exact opposite is true. Jesus sought to empower His moral warriors to challenge and combat evil at every turn, and our battle today is in the political and cultural landscape, because that is where our deficits originate. The soul of our nation is at stake.

Isn't it high time that Christians stepped up on behalf of the culture and our shared future? Blessed are the meek, those who wield power under control, for they will inherit the earth."

Blessed are the meek, for they shall inherit the earth.
—Matthew 5:5

Discussion Questions

1. Describe the last time you became upset with someone at church. Was it over a doctrinal issue, or was it over a preference? How did you respond?

2. What are some preferences that you are passionate about? Can you see how the devil could use your passion to create division?

3. Do you struggle with speaking out when God is leading you to be quiet? How can you use what you learned in this chapter to correct this?

4. Why do you think it is easy to argue over preferences but remain silent over biblical truths?

5. Give an example of a time you had to be gentle.

6. Give an example of a time you had to be a giant.

7. Give an example of a time you were balanced, a gentle giant.

To see a video from the author with more thoughts on this topic, and enjoy more resources, please visit: www.beingthebelieving.com.

CHAPTER FOUR

A Healthy Hunger
with Kathy Garver

Blessed are those who hunger and thirst for righteousness,
for they shall be satisfied.
                              —Matthew 5:6

At the outset, there are a few issues that we need to address with this text, the first being the language in both of the words, "hunger" and "thirst." An interpretation that more accurately reflects the original Greek verb tense would read something like: "Blessed are those who are hunger*ing* and thirst*ing* for righteousness."

This text is not speaking of a one-time event or a past occurrence, but a constant longing—a deep, insatiable, continuous craving for righteousness.

Many folks will never experience what it is really like to hunger and thirst because with many of us the only decision we have to make, in regard to food, is whether or not to supersize our next meal.

In 1987, I went through a period of time that provided me with the unique opportunity to appreciate the meaning behind this verse, for I had such a sense of hunger and thirst. I was stationed on the United States Coast Guard Cutter Sweetbrier out of Cordova, Alaska. The scope of duty for this ship and her crew was to provide search and rescue, aids to navigation, law enforcement patrols, and international intervention.

Jesus wants to get us to the point that we are hungering and thirsting to the degree that He is all that we think about; all that we need.

Since our missions were carried out in the Prince William Sound and the Bering Sea, we all had to go through Cold Water Survival School, which included spending time on an uninhabited island.

We were dropped a couple hundred yards off the beach in our leaking "waterproof" Gumby suits and were required to swim to shore, conduct a perimeter search, get dry, establish a camp in our groups of four to six, build a shelter, compile resources, and survive until we were "rescued" a couple of days later.

This training was designed to replicate either a sinking ship or man overboard scenario. And, since these situations could not be prepared for, we were forbidden to bring anything with us that we normally would not have on our person during the course of an average day. Our group found out later that some of the other groups smuggled cans of tuna, lighters, knives and even tobacco onto the island. Our group followed the rules to the T and had nothing but our wet clothes that became stiff as boards during the night. In fact, I used my Gumby suit as part of the roof for our shelter!

Those who desire a relationship with God must come to the place in their lives where they need *a relationship with God.*

Toward the end of this training, I had consumed water from my wrung-out socks and ate the rotten flesh off a washed-up dead fish I found on a rock. I can tell you that for the first time in my life, I was really hungering and thirsting. I had gotten to the point that my entire focus was on finding something to eat and drink; nothing else mattered.

That is the theme of this text. Jesus wants to get us to the point where we are hungering and thirsting to the degree that He is all that we think about, and that nothing else matters. He wants us to have a deep, insatiable, and continuous craving.

What are we to hunger and thirst for? Righteousness! What is righteousness? Well, it's really not that simple. In fact, scholars have debated this question as it pertains to this text for years. Some think this is speaking of:

Salvation Given to Us by God

Some interpret this text to mean salvation given to us by God. That would seem to confirm the thought brought out in Matthew 5:3, which says, "Blessed are the poor in spirit, for theirs is the kingdom of heaven." Those who desire a relationship with God must come to the place in their lives where they *need* a relationship with God.

There will be a time when our Father will return, fix everything broken, and make right everything that is wrong.

This is desperation, a hungering and thirsting. It's the same hungering and thirsting that caused a previously obstinate eighteenth-century congregation to cry out for mercy in response to the fire-and-brimstone preaching of Jonathan Edwards,[27] as if fearing that at any moment the floor would open up wide for hell to receive them.

This is the same hungering and thirsting that caused me to double-time down the aisle of a church in Massachusetts in 1990, under the full conviction of the Holy Spirit of God that I was a sinner in need of a Savior.

This is the same hungering and thirsting that has been experienced by multitudes who have grown weary and tired of never being satisfied, ultimately crying out to Jesus and discovering the joy that comes from burdens lifted, forgiveness offered and receiving a life full of purpose and meaning. So, *salvation* certainly seems to be a fitting interpretation of our word *righteousness*.

Another thought of what this righteousness could be is:

Standing Given for Us Through Christ

Others interpret this verse to address the Christian's standing, or position, given through the sacrificial and redemptive work of Jesus Christ. These scholars believe the hungering and thirsting to be eschatological in nature—causing us to look ahead and be confident through this life, knowing that there will be a time when our Father will return, fix everything broken, and make right everything that is wrong. This interpretation of the text speaks more to *standing*—our position—than to salvation.

The older I get and the more I study, the more I realize how little I know. But, I know who Jesus is, what He did, where He is, and who I am because of it all—my position or standing. I know that there is coming a day when my heart will stop beating, my eyes will close, my breath will leave, and those who are left behind will bury my body in the ground, throwing up a gravestone marking the place where many think it all ends. But meanwhile, up in heaven, there will be some rejoicing going on, for another sinner has come home. The angels will be swirling, the saints dancing, the greats shouting, my Savior standing—oh what a glorious day that will be!

And, knowing these things to be true, I am hungering and thirsting for that final day when the clouds are rolled back like a scroll, the trumpet resounds and my Lord descends; even so it will be well with my soul![28]

So, I can certainly see why some interpret this word to speak of our standing through Christ, yet still other theologians and scholars believe this righteousness speaks of:

Sanctification Given by Us for This World

Lastly, many interpret this text to speak of the sanctification given by us for this world. This is where I land in the interpretation of the word "righteousness" in the text. *Sanctification* simply means to set apart for a special purpose, and the process of becoming holy.[29] And, boy, do we need more believers who have an insatiable hungering and thirsting for the things of God, to be more and more conformed to His image, and set apart to become holy!

Never getting over your salvation or losing the wonder of it all is the meaning behind our hungering and thirsting for righteousness.

You see, sanctification is not a one-time event that takes place during salvation but a process. This is why the apostle Paul admonishes, in Romans 12:1–2, to "present your bodies as a living sacrifice, holy and acceptable to God, which is your spiritual worship. Do not be conformed to this world, but be transformed by the renewal of your mind, that by testing you may discern what is the will of God, what is good and acceptable and perfect." So, salvation comes *from* God, and sanctification comes *from* us and *from* God, since we have neither the desire nor the power to be sanctified apart from the work of the Holy Spirit. This is what it means to have a hungering and thirsting for righteousness.

And the result of not having a hungering and thirsting for righteousness is hypocrisy owned by a professing Christian; hence, someone with a desecrated testimony. Think back with me and remember when you first came into a relationship with Jesus Christ. If you were anything like me:

- You could not read and hear enough from the Word of God.

- You could not stay away from the house of God, coming every time the doors were opened. You couldn't imagine a time when your church family was meeting, and you were not in the center of it all.

- You were telling everyone you met about the glorious transformation that had occurred in your life.

- You spent more time praying than watching TV.

- You were on committees, working with children, teaching youth, helping on church workdays, going on visitations, filling up the offering plate, planning that next mission trip, loving God and loving people!

- You were so consumed by the things of God, obsessed with the Word of God, and in desperate love with the people of God, that it was like you could never get enough; your cup was constantly running over.

That is what it means, hungering and thirsting for righteousness. Gypsy Smith, a great evangelist in the early twentieth century, was once asked for the secret of his powerful and lasting ministry. He replied, "I never lost the wonder of it all."[30] Never getting over your salvation or losing the wonder of it all is the meaning behind our hungering and thirsting for righteousness.

When you cease to hunger and thirst after righteousness, you desecrate your testimony, trade power for hypocrisy, and become gospel-useless.

Tragically, so many Christians who used to be in the race are now in the ditch of life, no longer hungering and thirsting for righteousness. This is nothing new. The nation of Israel, after experiencing a supernatural release from their condition of slavery in Egypt, spent years wandering in the wilderness, motivated by the temptation to view the past through a distorted lens that presented it as better than their current situation. Their past then became tethered to their present, which crippled their potential and delayed their journey to joy. In essence, they were insatiably restless as they were looking to the wrong things for satisfaction. How true of our current restless culture, a culture where so many are looking to the wrong things to provide satisfaction: power, popularity, prestige, position, and promotion, all while being motivated by a desire for acceptance, approval, and even love. All these things are worthy and attainable, but they cannot be found outside of a relationship with God.

Oh, friend, the need for you to hunger and thirst after righteousness is much bigger than you. Yes, God will bless you if you are hungering and thirsting after Him, but know this: you are not an island, and your life does affect those around you.

Israel's King David knew this concept, which is why he was hungering and thirsting after righteousness and known as a man after God's own heart (Acts 13:22). There are certainly benefits to having an insatiable appetite for the things of God.

But here is the warning: when you cease to hunger and thirst after righteousness, you desecrate your testimony, trade power for hypocrisy, and become gospel-useless. And when that happens, you lose joy, power, peace, and victory in your life at best, and become the excuse others use to reject the gospel of Jesus Christ, at worst.

"Christians" have unintentionally steered others away from Christ by promoting the creation or growth of more religions and cults than anyone else.

In the sixth century, a young man was born into this world, his dad dying before he was born and his mom dying when he was but seven years old. He was then raised by his grandfather, who also died, which left him in the care of his uncle. In spite of this dysfunctional and unstable background, he became a young man of great reputation: honest, hardworking, driven, and passionate. He would go off every year in isolation to a cave, praying and fasting from dusk till dawn.

It was during one of these trips that an "angel" came to him, declared him a messenger of God and told him to start a new religion. He ran home scared and told his wife and family to cover him for protection.[31] When he questioned this "angel's" message from God, for him to become a messenger and start a new religion, his wife brought him to her cousin, who was known as a Christian savant, someone who had a reputation for being informed and educated in Christianity. This "Christian" confirmed this man's calling, declared him to be a true prophet of God, and encouraged him to start a new religion.[32] This religion is now the second-largest, and fastest growing, religion in the world. I am talking about Islam and its founder Muhammad.

In 1869, Mahatma Gandhi was born in India and eventually became a leader and voice of the third-largest world religion, Hinduism. Had he been exposed to genuine Christianity, he would have had the potential to influence and convert millions. In fact, there was a time in his life that he researched and investigated other religions, ultimately embracing some aspects of another religion, Sikhism. He is often credited with saying, after his research on Christianity: "I like your Christ; I do not like your Christians. Your Christians are so unlike your Christ."

In 1930, a very intelligent man was born in Chicago. He had a troubled upbringing, dropped out of high school, ran away and joined a carnival. He was exposed to, and even considered, many religions, even dabbling in the occult; he was what we would call a seeker. He was drawn more to Christianity than to any other religion and even started playing the organ for traveling preachers on Sundays at the carnival where he worked.

Of Christianity he wrote, "On Saturday night I would see men lusting after half-naked girls dancing at the carnival, and on Sunday morning when I was playing the organ for tent-show evangelists at the other end of the carnival lot, I would see these same men sitting in the pew with their wives and children, asking God to forgive them and purge them of carnal desires. And the next Saturday night they'd be back at the carnival or some other place of indulgence. I knew then that the Christian Church thrives on hypocrisy, and that man's carnal nature will win out!"[33]

What would you be like if you were hungering and thirsting after righteousness?

Disillusioned and frustrated with the blatant hypocrisy thriving in Christianity, he decided to write a book and start his own church. His name was Anton LaVey; the book he wrote was *The Satanic Bible;* and the church he started was the Church of Satan

That is why I stated that Christians have unintentionally, indirectly, promoted more religions and cults than anyone else has.

But not all cases are as blatant and apparent. What about the "Christian" parent who is more committed to sports on the Sabbath than to church? Or the "Christian" who honks and yells their way through traffic while displaying a fish magnet on their car? Or the employee who tells inappropriate jokes around the water cooler, gossips about their demanding boss, complains about every ache and pain, yet sings in their church choir every Sunday celebrating the power and presence of God?

While not seemingly as destructive as writing a book called *The Satanic Bible,* are these not examples of "Christians" who point people away from Christ by lives that declare Jesus is not enough?

What would this world be like if more Christians were hungering and thirsting after righteousness? What would *you* be like if you were hungering and thirsting after righteousness?

Satisfaction Given in Us Through the Holy Spirit

This is the message humanity needs so desperately to hear today. When you hunger and thirst for Christ, He will fill you. This world does not get this. Oh, there are many who are hungering and thirsting today, just not for the right things.

We hunger and thirst for things like drugs, relation-ships, alcohol, family, hobbies, education, money, approval, health, vanity, position, careers, food, power, praise, and pleasure. Never forget; God designed us to have a hungering and a thirsting. According to Ecclesias-tes 3:11, God placed eternity in our hearts; it's in our very DNA! God designed us to hunger and thirst after Him; God designed us with a GPS to guide us to His love. This is not new. Nor is it new for humanity to hunger and thirst after something other than God.

God designed us to hunger and thirst after Him; God designed us with a GPS to guide us to His love

Satan was hungering and thirsting to rise into the heav-ens and become God. God humbled him. According to the account in Isaiah 14, Satan had a desire to rise into heaven, usurp God, set up his own throne, and rule as God. This was a hunger and thirst for *power* that was never satisfied. This is something that remains a plague upon this earth; an issue of control. Marriages break up, jobs are lost, and churches divide and, at times, close their doors, all over the battle for control.

King Nebuchadnezzar looked down at the great king-dom of Babylon and declared, "Is not this great Babylon, which I have built by my mighty power as a royal resi-dence for the glory of my majesty?" (Daniel 4:30). God humbled him. This was a hunger and thirst for *praise* that was never satisfied.

Again, this is another issue that has many disillusioned in a world where the wells of praise have run dry. While the desire to receive praise may not inherently be evil, the *who* or *what* we seek that praise from can be. Hungering and thirsting after God means that we seek our praise from a sole source; God, and He is very willing to give it. The Bible says that God is a "rewarder of those that diligently seek Him" (Hebrews 11:6 NKJV). Therefore, if praise is what you are after, hunger and thirst (seek) for God and you will be satisfied.

The story of the rich young fool, as taught by Jesus, depicted a man who thought life was summed up in the statement "eat, drink and be merry" (Luke 12:19). God humbled him. This was a hunger and thirst for *pleasure* that was never satisfied.

This last example is perhaps the most troublesome in our current culture, with most of our resources and pursuits being dedicated to this very thing, pleasure. According to the Bureau of Labor Statistics 2016 Consumer Expenditure Survey, apart from housing, food, transportation, and medical expenditures, Americans spend most of their budget on pleasures: alcohol, tobacco, television, pornography, going out to eat, mobile devices, personal luxury care, vacations, and other miscellaneous non-essentials.[34] This is all done in the pursuit of pleasure, what feels good.

All the while, God offers pleasures this world can't touch, and while God does not require a certain percentage of your budget to obtain this pleasure, He does demand your willingness to put all your pleasure eggs in His basket.

As I look at the above examples of a life hungering and thirsting after things like power, praise and pleasure, I recognize there was a time when this was descriptive of my life. I remember clearly, a few months before I became a follower of Christ, that I had this overwhelming sense of a void in my life. After one long night of tossing and turning, I got out of bed, grabbed a piece of paper and a pencil, and took an inventory of my life. When I finished, everything appeared to be good, yet I still felt there was something missing, an undetermined and unrecognized void. I had power, praise, and pleasure, yet inexplicably remained unsatisfied. It was only after I came to Christ that I discovered what true satisfaction was.

In attacking the prosperity gospel, John Piper has pointed out that even if we are involved in a car accident that flings our child through the windshield to die in a pool of blood on the street, Jesus Christ can be enough. That is why we should hunger and thirst after righteousness, as it is only through this act that we can be satisfied, completely satisfied, no matter what.[35]

My wife, Laurie, grew up enjoying the celebrated sitcom *A Family Affair.* One of those characters, Kathy Garver, who played Cissy, has become a friend of mine in recent years. This Beatitude is her favorite and she has come to the conclusion that hungering and thirsting for God is not a one-time event, but rather a lifelong journey of discovery. I will let her share those thoughts in her own words.

As Pastor McCracken has indicated earlier in *Being the Believing*, hunger and thirst is perhaps better read as hungering and thirsting for righteousness. That rendering puts each of us in a state of existing and in living from moment to moment. In that moment, we need to bask in the light of Jesus and using His luminescence to fulfill our need to be with God. In my opinion, righteousness and justice take on the cloak of sanctification by allowing us to use that light to help illuminate the paths of others. And in show business, so many of the fans, actors, and producers I meet definitely need to have their lights turned on. They need to be shown the wonderful light that exists in each one of us.

Show business is not an easy business. It is fraught with disappointments, frustration, and people breaking contracts of faith. Recently, I had an experience in which I had worked for almost eight years helping a "friend" to get a movie made, introducing him to agents, potential investors, and actors. I was always promised a role in the film, and every time we talked, my friend would regale me with tales of what my character would do, how she would react to other characters, and scenes that might be incorporated into the movie—and then into the sequel of the movie. He would tell me that the accompanying series about real estate would be directed by a very experienced director with over 590 TV episodes to his credit. Indeed, this director does have all those episodes to his credit. I had not taken any money for all the time I had worked with my friend on casting, funding, and ideas to get his movie made.

One month ago, the film was finally funded by those to whom I had introduced my friend, but the director demanded that my role be filled by someone else, and he had it in his contract that he had the right to choose. So, there was no role for me in a movie where I had worked very hard for it to be produced and no part or producer's credit. Was this fair? Was this righteous? Certainly not. But it was not justice I sought. I was seeking, with the gift of fortitude, a way to stay and be successful in my career because every time a disappointment comes my way, I am patient and fulfilled with God's Spirit.

This acceptance of God's grace and fulfilled by Him has allowed me to have greater recognition of projects that better spread my understanding of God and belief to others. After this experience, my life is now filled with God's Spirit as I begin work on a new series, two new movies, and with the joyful anticipation of two new cruises on which I will sail with fellow actors and friends. I hungered and thirsted for God's Spirit to fill me since I know that is the correct way to sate my hunger and thirst. I am able to share this Spirit in more projects that will come my way. With new friends, fans, and peers, there will be a way for them to ignite their own inner lights. And that is right and just.

Blessed are those who hunger and thirst for righteousness, for they shall be satisfied.
—Matthew 5:6

Discussion Questions

1. Why do you think God uses the analogy of "hungering and thirsting"?

2. Being honest, what do you hunger and thirst for the most in this life?

3. Is there anything that comes between you and Jesus? Anything that, at times, dominates your time, attention, and resources?

4. Has there ever been anything in your life that used to give you great pleasure that you have since traded up for Jesus? How does Jesus compare to that past pleasure?

To see a video from the author with more thoughts on this topic, and more, please visit www.beingthebelieving.com/videos.

CHAPTER FIVE

Compassion in Action
with Ann-Marie Murrell

Blessed are the merciful, for they shall receive mercy.
—Matthew 5:7

While the first four Beatitudes deal with our relationship with God, these next four deal with our relationships with each other. This is where so many professing Christians are missing the mark.

Many think they can have a great relationship with God and never make the connection with other believers or even His church. It has been said that you can't love Christ and hate His church; loving Christ and His church are married concepts that will always remain inseparable.

To understand the Beatitudes is to understand that what God gives us is not meant to be kept to ourselves but given out to others. Christianity is an outpouring of an indwelling. In other words, the first four Beatitudes tell us that we have been given eternal life, comfort, power, and satisfaction, and the first thing that God tells us to do with these glorious gifts is to show mercy to others.

Mercy Is Foreign to the World and Will Not Be Rewarded by the World

Mercy is not something that comes naturally in our world. In the Roman culture in which this sermon was given, mercy was not a popular concept that was believed to improve society, but rather a weakness to be eradicated. One Roman philosopher called mercy "the disease of the soul." It was in this setting that when a child was born, the baby would be lifted up to the father and if he thought the child was healthy and attractive, he would give a "thumbs up" and the child would live. If he thought the child ugly, too loud or unhealthy, he would give a "thumbs down" and the child would be put to death.[36]

Mercy has always been foreign to the world and not rewarded by the world.

And in this merciless culture a Roman citizen, for any reason, could kill and bury a slave without any consequence. Additionally, a husband could put his wife to death without fear of retribution.[37]

It was in this dark culture, void of mercy, that Jesus stated, "Blessed are the merciful, for they shall receive mercy" (Matthew 5:7). Not much has changed from the culture of Roman history to our current American culture as we are giving a "thumbs down" to over one million unborn babies each year in America and calling it abortion.

Domestic violence is the leading cause of injury to women between the ages of 15 and 44 in the United States, more than car accidents, muggings, and rapes combined.[38] Even in our schools, a no-mercy culture seems to be prevailing, evidenced by 5.4 million students skipping school every year for fear of bullying.[39]

We are not called to enable the greedy but to empower the needy.

Mercy has always been foreign to the world and not rewarded by the world. Jesus made the lame to walk again, and He caused the blind to see. He brought the dead to life and hearing to the deaf and reached out to the outcasts and the untouchables. He sought out the tax collectors, the degenerates, the immoral, the prostitutes, the drunkards, the despised, and the rejected, and praise God, He even reached out to the likes of you and me.

Jesus shocked the culture of the day by His many displays of great mercy, and those acts of mercy were rarely received with gratefulness, but instead rejected with hostility. He was shamed, had stones thrown at Him, and was accused of being demon-possessed, drunk and crazy. And yet, He never stopped, rather He continued to display relentless mercy to all.

Jesus showed us by example that mercy is foreign to the world and rejected by the world. If they rejected Jesus and His mercy, they will reject you and your mercy.

> *If the world hates you, know that it has hated me before it hated you.*
>
> **—John 15:18**

Yet, we must continue to be agents of mercy to those *around us* if we are to receive mercy from the Father *above us*.

Mercy Is Not a Feeling, but Compassion in Action

The *Preaching the Word* commentary on Matthew explains this "compassion in action" principle by the story of a nineteenth-century preacher who happened across a friend whose horse had just been accidentally killed.[40]

While the crowd of onlookers expressed empty words of sympathy, the preacher stepped forward and said to the loudest sympathizer, "I am sorry five pounds. How much are you sorry?" And then he passed his hat around to the crowd. True mercy demands action. True mercy always translates to action; this is compassion in action.

Let's break this "compassion in action" down to three areas: *meeting right physical needs, holding a right attitude*, and *being spiritually mature*.

Meeting the Right Physical Needs

Notice I qualified this idea of meeting physical needs with the use of the word "right." We are not called to enable the greedy but to empower the needy; to feed the hungry, visit the sick, provide for the orphans and widows, clothe the naked, and visit the imprisoned. Yet, not all people seeking help should receive the specific help requested.

Years ago, I was standing in line at a local restaurant after church with some friends, waiting for a table. We were approached by a homeless man who was seeking money for "food." Wanting to set the pastoral example before other Christians, I obliged and gave the man a twenty-dollar bill. He happily took my money, and I was feeling pretty good about this deed until my eyes followed this man right to the liquor store across the street! I left the restaurant, crossed the street, and found him at the counter with a large bottle of cheap whiskey, handing the clerk my twenty-dollar bill. Needless to say, I left him penniless at the counter.

While we are to meet the needs of those around us as best we can with the resources God has provided, we must qualify those needs with the wisdom and discernment God has given. Again, we are not called to enable the greedy but to empower the needy.

Holding a Right Attitude

John MacArthur, in his commentary on Matthew, states:

> Mercy does not hold a grudge, harbor resentment, capitalize on another's failure or weakness, or publicize another's sin. On a great table at which he fed countless hundreds of people, Augustine inscribed, "Whoever thinks that he is able to nibble at the life of absent friends, must know that he's unworthy of this table." The vindictive, heartless, and indifferent are not subjects of Christ; they show they have passed Christ's kingdom. When they pass need by on the other side, as the priest and the Levite did in the story of the Good Samaritan, they show they have passed Christ by.[41]

God never leaves us where He finds us.

While it is crucial that we are found faithful in being merciful, we must always be certain that we are just as faithful in having a right attitude. So many times, we have an ulterior motive or personal agenda behind our acts of mercy. While we may be showing mercy, we must be sure that our good deeds are not for recognition, worldly reward, or human reciprocation, but for the glory of our Father and for Him alone.

Being Spiritually Mature

This aspect is broken down into three parts: *pity, provocation and prayer*, all of which involve God's children doing more than just crying out, losing sleep, or even feeling bad—again highlighting the truth that mercy is much more than a feeling or emotion. Mercy, true mercy, always fleshes out as action, which comes from spiritual maturity. One of the great truths of Christianity is that God never leaves us where He finds us, meaning we can be maturing every day, having the potential of daily growth. This growth is marked by the increased mercy we show to others *around us* based on the growing power *within us*.

Mercy Is Shown Through Pity

Pity can have a negative connotation in our culture. The word has become associated with condescension and looking down on others while simultaneously thinking more highly of ourselves because at least our situation isn't that bad! Nobody wants to be pitied.

This definition from the Oxford Dictionary, however, puts the word *pity* back in its original, intended context: "The feeling of sorrow and compassion caused by the sufferings and misfortunes of others."[42] This certainly ties into the second Beatitude: "Blessed are those who mourn, for they shall be comforted."

When we see people who are hurting and struggling in sin, our response should be one of compassionate action. Augustine stated, "If I weep for the body from which the soul is departed, should I not weep for the soul from which God is departed?"[43]

I have been to hundreds of funerals, and if memory serves correctly, every one of them, without exception, involved people crying over the body of someone who died. Mercy is displayed in the believer's life when they cry more for those who will be missed in heaven than those whom they miss on earth. Mercy is shown through genuine, heartfelt compassion for the sufferings and misfortunes of others.

Mercy Is Shown Through Provocation

I believe many do not come to church because they are living in sin, and the minister, the music, and the membership all represent God. That means conflict, and conflict is most often intentionally avoided.

The greatest mercy you can show to someone is presenting them with the gospel, even though doing so may provoke conflict. If you ignore the Spirit's prompting to share the gospel with someone who needs to hear it, due to fear of provoking conflict, you are denying them an opportunity to receive salvation.

Be bold, passionate, and proactive. Don't be so afraid of conflict that you refuse to discuss the reality of sin and the need for a Savior in Jesus Christ.

Mercy Is Shown Through Prayer

MacArthur gauges it this way: "Our mercy can be measured by our prayer for the unsaved and for Christians who are walking in disobedience."[44]

Again, this goes back to Matthew 5:4: "Blessed are those who mourn, for they shall be comforted." Mourn over what? Your sin and the sins of those around you. When was the last time you really cried out in prayer for the lost and the disobedient, knowing they were hurting the very heart of God, and knowing they face an eternal separation from Him?

Oh, how far we have come in American church culture. There was a time when the church would gather every Wednesday night, collapse at the altar, and cry out in prayer for the unsaved and the backslidden. Wood was warped and carpet stained as the mourning of congregations resonated within the sanctuary of God.

Prayer is not about what we get but Who we get to know.

We need some more old-fashioned church services where mercy is shown through prayer. We need some old-school, confession-and-repentance time of prayer where we are getting right with God and each other and, through the power of unity, getting this world back to a right relationship with God. We should not be concerned with the position of the pulpit before people but the position of people before God.

Remember 2 Chronicles 7:14: "If my people who are called by my name humble themselves, and pray and seek my face and turn from their wicked ways, then I will hear from heaven and will forgive their sin and heal their land." This world is sick and in need of healing, and we have the cure. The answer is not to be found in the schoolhouse, courthouse, police house, and certainly not the White House, but in God's house, with His people displaying a merciful God by being merciful. In that vein, our church has set aside a room for that purpose; for Christians to spend time in prayer; not primarily asking God to make our lives better or more comfortable, but rather that His will would be done in and through our very lives. I believe that when we understand prayer is not about *what we get* but *Who we get to know*, miracles will happen.

Mercy Is Anchored to Forgiveness Rooted in Christ

Mercy is anchored to forgiveness rooted in Christ. When I fell at the cross at twenty-one years old, I was a wicked, vile, worldly, self-consumed, and flesh-driven sinner, deserving of jail in this life and hell in the next. And the truth is, I still struggle with sin. But I am blessed to have experienced the forgiveness of a holy God through a loving Savior. I am not better than those who are still in the darkness of their sin, but I am better off. I am better off because I have received the mercy, love, and forgiveness offered by Jesus Christ and have been made His child forever because I repented of my sin.

I can think of no better illustration that mercy is anchored to forgiveness than the story of Corrie ten Boom. In an excerpt from her book, *The Hiding Place,* Corrie relates the following story:

> It was in a church in Munich that I saw him—a balding, heavyset man in a gray overcoat, a brown felt hat clutched between his hands. People were filing out of the basement room where I had just spoken, moving along the rows of wooden chairs to the door at the rear. It was 1947 and I had come from Holland to defeated Germany with the message that God forgives.
>
> It was the truth they needed most to hear in that bitter, bombed-out land, and I gave them my favorite mental picture. Maybe because the sea is never far from a Hollander's mind, I liked to think that that's where forgiven sins were thrown. "When we confess our sins," I said, "God casts them into the deepest ocean, gone forever...."
>
> The solemn faces stared back at me, not quite daring to believe. There were never questions after a talk in Germany in 1947. People stood up in silence, in silence collected their wraps, in silence left the room.
>
> And that's when I saw him, working his way forward against the others. One moment I saw the overcoat and the brown hat; the next, a blue uniform and a visored cap with its skull and crossbones. It came back with a rush: the huge room with its harsh overhead lights; the pathetic pile of dresses and shoes in the center of the floor; the shame of walking naked past this man. I could see my sister's frail form ahead of me, ribs sharp beneath the parchment skin. Betsie, how thin you were!
>
> [Betsie and I had been arrested for concealing Jews in our home during the Nazi occupation of Holland; this

man had been a guard at Ravensbruck concentration camp where we were sent.]

Now he was in front of me, hand thrust out: "A fine message, Fräulein! How good it is to know that, as you say, all our sins are at the bottom of the sea!"

And I, who had spoken so glibly of forgiveness, fumbled in my pocketbook rather than take that hand. He would not remember me, of course—how could he remember one prisoner among those thousands of women?

But I remembered him and the leather crop swinging from his belt. I was face-to-face with one of my captors and my blood seemed to freeze.

"You mentioned Ravensbruck in your talk," he was saying, "I was a guard there." No, he did not remember me.

"But since that time," he went on, "I have become a Christian. I know that God has forgiven me for the cruel things I did there, but I would like to hear it from your lips as well. Fräulein," again the hand came out—"will you forgive me?"

And I stood there—I whose sins had again and again been forgiven—and could not forgive. Betsie had died in that place—could he erase her slow terrible death simply for the asking?

It could not have been many seconds that he stood there—hand held out—but to me it seemed hours as I wrestled with the most difficult thing I had ever had to do.

For I had to do it—I knew that. The message that God forgives has a prior condition: that we forgive those who have injured us. "If you do not forgive men their trespasses," Jesus says, "neither will your Father in heaven forgive your trespasses."

I knew it not only as a commandment of God, but as a daily experience. Since the end of the war I had had a home in Holland for victims of Nazi brutality. Those who were able to forgive their former enemies were able also to return to the outside world and rebuild their lives, no matter what the physical scars. Those who nursed their bitterness remained invalids. It was as simple and as horrible as that.

And still I stood there with the coldness clutching my heart. But forgiveness is not an emotion—I knew that too. Forgiveness is an act of the will, and the will can function regardless of the temperature of the heart. "... Help!" I prayed silently. "I can lift my hand. I can do that much. You supply the feeling."

And so woodenly, mechanically, I thrust my hand into the one stretched out to me. And as I did, an incredible thing took place. The current started in my shoulder, raced down my arm, sprang into our joined hands. And then this healing warmth seemed to flood my whole being, bringing tears to my eyes.

"I forgive you, brother!" I cried. "With all my heart!"

For a long moment we grasped each other's hands, the former guard and the former prisoner. I had never known God's love so intensely, as I did then.[45]

If we have received unmerited forgiveness from God, then we must give that forgiveness freely to others. For the truth is, it is not our mercy we are to keep; it is His mercy we are to give.

Mercy Is Rewarded by the Faithfulness of God

Blessed are the merciful, for they shall receive mercy.
                                        —Matthew 5:7

This is the only Beatitude that speaks of getting what you give. Not from the world, but from God! If you show mercy, you will receive mercy. What does this mean? The other Beatitudes seem pretty clear: when we are poor in spirit, we receive the kingdom of heaven. When we mourn, we receive comfort. When we display meekness, we inherit the earth. And when we hunger and thirst for righteousness, we are promised to be filled. But show mercy and receive mercy? This means that you will benefit from the faithfulness of God.

If you allow God to demonstrate His mercy *through you* by showing mercy to those *around you,* you will receive mercy from the One *above you* by His assurance *within you.*

You see, when you show mercy, you are demonstrating that you have a power within that can only come from without. Hence, we are able to experience a two-fold blessing, one that is internal and one that is external:

An Internal Blessing: Assurance of Salvation

This is a promise from God, friend, a promise that can change your life. Showing mercy is an indication that you are saved and secure so that you can be sure.

Do you have days that you doubt? Days you struggle? Nights when you wonder if God has left you, forgotten you, given up on you? Times when your feelings seem to trump your beliefs?

If you allow God to demonstrate His mercy *through you* by showing mercy to those *around you*, you will receive mercy from the One *above you* by His assurance *within you*.

There is no higher joy and no better comfort than being able to lay down at night—even in the midst of the doubting and accusing voices from the world, the devil, and even the flesh—only to have a text like this penetrate that doubt with the wonderful truth that you are His and He is yours.

An External Blessing: Access to Salvation

This world needs the joy and comfort that you have received from God. And in this merciless culture in which we live, there is no greater stage on which to present the gospel than through mercy shown to those in need. We must not be conformed to a world that is full of anger and hate marked by constant division, racism, protests, and picket lines; rather we should understand the only potential for true change lies solely in the lap of the gospel.

Stop inviting people to church and start inviting people to become the church.

The truth is, as believers, we all have the unique

opportunity to display mercy to those around us by letting out what is in us, for the glory of the One above us, that all would come to the saving knowledge of the One who died for all of us.

Before we move on, let me add a warning to never replace inviting people to Christ with inviting people to church. How about we stop inviting people *to* church and start inviting people to *become* the church? A church can't forgive, change or save anyone, only Christ can do that. Showing mercy is giving people what they need, and what people need the most is help from the only One able to help—not a church and not a religion. People need the Lord.

I met my next friend at a convention two years ago. Ann-Marie Murrell, an actress, political activist, and author who knows what showing mercy is all about. Ann-Marie gave up a lucrative career in Hollywood to care for her parents in Texas, a sacrificial act of mercy that ended up changing Ann-Marie's life. I will let her share in her own words:

> To the chagrin of six generations of ancestors, I left Texas when I was twenty and headed for Hollywood to pursue an acting career.
>
> After spending most of my life as an actress, public speaker, co-author, and all kinds of public-eye things, in 2016 I was diagnosed with Multiple Sclerosis. I'd already been misdiagnosed with fibromyalgia, so I knew something was wrong with me. I constantly struggled to keep up, only able to do 'so much' before crashing into that ever-present

wall. I couldn't imagine things getting worse, but as so often happens when you say that, they did.

In 2017, my sister Lisa and I realized our elderly parents needed full-time care. Because of her job, Lisa couldn't handle things on her own, so there was only one solution: I needed to move to Texas to help take care of our parents.

I was torn in half. I would have to leave my beautiful house on the hill, my son and daughter-in-law who lived a few miles away, and my husband, who had to stay and work. But ultimately it came down to who needed me most—and that's when I did what I always do: I turned to God and asked Him to guide me. So ultimately Jesus brought me back to Texas.

In the process my husband and I divorced but that was inevitable. We both realized we were never really on the same path and neither were our priorities.

Ever since, maybe for the first time in my life, I've been on God's path, not mine. And perhaps because of this He's been leading me to some of the best people I've ever known—old friends and new. Best of all, my son and his wife recently moved to Texas, too!

Despite my physical struggles and some of the darkest, saddest times surrounding my family and me, I've never been happier. The holes I didn't even know were there have been filled up being back home in Texas.

Thank   you,   Jesus—YOU   did   that.   Amen.

Blessed are the merciful, for they shall receive mercy.
—Matthew 5:7

Discussion Questions

1. Has there ever been a time when you were misunderstood, maligned, misrepresented, mistreated, attacked, lied about, lied to, or abused? What was your response? Did you show mercy, or did you attack and hold a grudge? Did you allow the situation to *better* who you are or cause you to be *bitter*?

2. Why is it hard to show mercy to the undeserving?

3. Explain how evangelism is the greatest display of mercy. Why do we not do it more?

To see a video from the author with more thoughts on this topic, and to enjoy more resources, please visit: www.beingthebelieving.com.

CHAPTER SIX

Purity for Surety
with Jenn Gotzon Chandler

Blessed are the pure in heart, for they shall see God.
—Matthew 5:8

Kent Hughes, in his commentary on the Sermon on the Mount, relates the story of Anna Mae Pennica, a sixty-two-year-old woman who had been blind since birth. At age 47, she married a man she met in Braille class, and for the first fifteen years of their marriage, he did the seeing for both of them until he completely lost his vision to retinitis pigmentosa.[46]

Mrs. Pennica had never seen the green of spring or the blue of a winter sky. Yet, because she had grown up in a loving, supportive family, she never felt resentful about her disability and always exuded a remarkably cheerful spirit.

Then in October 1981, Dr. Thomas Pettit of the Jules Stein Eye Institute of the University of California at Los

Angeles performed surgery to remove the rare congenital cataracts from the lens of her left eye, and Mrs. Pennica saw for the first time ever!

She found that everything was "so much bigger and brighter" than she ever imagined. While she immediately recognized her husband and others that she had known well, other acquaintances were taller or shorter, heavier or skinnier than she had pictured them.

Oh, how many graces of God we often take for granted!

Since that day, Mrs. Pennica has hardly been able to wait to wake up in the morning, splash her eyes with water, put on her glasses and enjoy the changing morning light. Her vision is almost 20/30, good enough to pass a driver's test.

Can you even imagine? Oh, how many graces of God we often take for granted! Think what it must have been like to live for many years not seeing and then being able to watch the sunrise for the very first time? To enjoy the sunset on the ocean as birds fly by? Or to gaze into the eyes of your lover, wink at your child, or watch a football game?

Seeing is glorious; it is a miracle, really. Similarly, purity is all about seeing. However, it's not as much about God seeing us as it is about us seeing Him, us knowing and loving Him.

There are three truths that stick out to me as I consider our text: *a devotion to purity, the depth of purity,* and *our desire for purity.*

A Devotion to Purity

First of all, what is purity? Purity conveys several meanings: removing bacteria from water and alloy from metal, getting rid of mixed feelings to achieve clarity, and banishing evil in order to enjoy freedom.

So, purity would be getting to the point in your life where you have achieved clarity and focus on the things of God by banishing evil from your life, in order to enjoy the freedom in Christ that He longs for you to have.

When we fall in love with Jesus Christ, our lives are marked by that kind of love.

Do this and you will be assured a power-filled, victorious Christian life that will make a difference *in* this world by bringing the glory of God *to* this world!

I know what you are thinking, "You don't know the boss I have to work for, the issues we are battling at home, or the pain I experience every day of my life."

Wouldn't most of us like to put all of those things on the altar, kill them, put them in a locked box, bury them deep in the ground, and be able to walk away and live for Christ unhindered?

That is exactly what the Bible tells us to do every day! Galatians 5:24 says, "And those who belong to Christ Jesus have crucified the flesh with its passions and desires."

That means you have to get to the point where Matthew 5:4—"Blessed are those who mourn, for they shall be comforted"—is prevalent in your life. When we fall in love with Jesus Christ, our lives are marked by that kind of love. And when He hurts, we hurt. And what hurts Him the most is when our disobedience and sin prevents our lives from bringing Him glory. So, we must get angry at our sin, take it out to the woodshed, and beat it down, standing over it and declaring, "Today I will be serving my Lord, and there is no room for you!" then turn around and walk away in victory.

When D. L. Moody was in Ireland, an evangelist there told him, "The world has yet to see what God can do with a man fully consecrated to Him." On his return to the States, that line stuck with him.[47] We may each desire to be that man, woman, boy, or girl, fully committed to God, yet we each struggle to make it happen.

Even after a church service on a Sunday morning when we get a taste of glory—the sermon is powerful, the music inspirational, and the prayers and fellowship sweet—it does not take long to realize how weak we are, for even on our way home, the moment someone cuts us off in traffic and gives a hand gesture that does not mean we are number one, we lose it.

How, then? How can we remain pure and experience a close, intimate and powerful relationship with God in this flesh, surrounded by the darkness of this world? I believe the answer is found in the *kind* of purity to which we have a devotion. There are six types of purity: primal, created, positional, imputed, practical, and ultimate.

Primal Purity

This is a purity held only by God. Hinduism, the third-largest religion, tells of their god, Shiva, who is living on a holy mountain in Asia, doing Yoga, smoking marijuana, and having sex—and millions worship him.[48] The God of the Bible is pure. What does it mean that God is pure? It means:

- God is mercy, justice and love.

- God will never go back on His word.

- God will never get so fed up with you that He takes out His eraser and blots your name out of the Book of Life.

- The love of God never gives up and never runs out.

- Nothing catches God off guard or by surprise.

- It means there will *never* be a time, in any circumstance or trial, when you can look up into heaven and find God pacing the halls of glory, wringing His hands, wondering what to do next because He did not see *that* coming!

- God knows you better than anyone yet chooses to love you more than anyone else loves you.

- God will never grow weary of your life and move on to find someone else who can love Him more or serve Him better.

Primal purity means that when this life is over, and you get to glory and see God face to face, He will be everything and more than you have ever read or heard about; and on that day you will declare that it has been worth it all. That is *primal* purity.

Created Purity

This was the purity enjoyed by Adam and Eve before the fall. They were able to walk and talk with God in Eden without temptation or distraction. They were able to look into the eyes of God without fear and live free of guilt. This purity was lost when Adam and Eve chose to rebel and sin against God, when they chose their desire to be *like* God over their desire to *know* God.

Positional Purity

This is the purity achieved through salvation. When we make that decision to "confess with our mouths that Jesus is Lord and believe in our hearts that God raised him from the dead" (Romans 10:9), we become pure in position. In other words, as dark, evil, wicked, and unworthy as you are, after salvation, when you stand before God, He no longer sees that sin, but sees His Son, our Savior!

Imputed or Actual Purity

This is the purity spoken of by Paul when he stated in 2 Corinthians 5:17, "Therefore if anyone is in Christ, he is a new creation. The old has passed away; behold, the new has come." I love this text. I can now go back to my family and friends, who knew me before I met Christ, and say, "Remember that sinful, rebellious, and angry Tom that you used to know? The one that you tossed aside and predicted would end up dead or in jail? The one that you said would never make anything of himself? Well, have I got something to show you now! 'Behold, all things have become new' (NKJV)! Come and see the great things that Christ has done!"

I love the way the apostle Paul put it when he said that we are to "put on the Lord Jesus Christ" (Romans 13:14a). Now that I am wearing the righteousness of Jesus, I can declare that His righteousness looks pretty good on me! This is imputed, or actual, purity.

Practical Purity

This is how purity is played out in the everyday, mundane, routine life of the believer. This is the purity to which we need a devotion. It is also called *sanctification*. We need to be devoted to setting our lives apart for the glorious purpose of making Christ known to this world through a life dedicated and consecrated to, through, and for Him. This is a daily decision to yield to the plan God has for our lives instead of creating, maintaining, and protecting our own. It is a belief that God's plan will always be better than ours because God knows more than we do.

Ultimate Purity

This is the heavenly purity that all born-again believers will one day enjoy. This is the aspect of salvation that I am most looking forward to, although there are many aspects to heaven that the collective church celebrates in anticipation while on earth: the streets of gold, walls of jasper, foundation of precious stone and the gates of pearl; the angelic beings, the greats and the saints, the family and friends that are missed and the lives that were touched but remain unknown to us this side of eternity.

Ultimate purity goes much deeper than any of these things. Ultimate purity brings us into an aspect of our salvation that we have yet to experience: freedom from the confines of this sinful body! Freedom to focus on Jesus Christ, giving Him unadulterated worship from a completely pure heart of integrity, with no distractions, disruptions or deteriorations. A future where we will be able to walk and talk with Him with complete focus, free of shame, guilt, and fear. That is heaven: the Garden of Eden restored, and the curse cured. And that is the ultimate purity we will one day enjoy; but for now, our devotion needs to be aimed at practical purity.

David once declared, "Who shall ascend the hill of the LORD? And who shall stand in his holy place? He who has clean hands and a pure heart; who does not lifted up his soul to what is false and does not swear deceitfully" (Psalm 24:3–4).

Who can ascend into the hill of the Lord or stand in His holy place? Those with clean hands and a pure heart! If you desire more from your relationship with God, you must realize the scope of this purity, or:

The Depth of Purity

Remember the verse, "Blessed are the merciful, for they shall receive mercy" (Matthew 5:7). We must clothe the naked, feed the hungry, and provide for the orphans and widows, remembering that God has not called us to enable the greedy, but to empower the needy. Having clean hands is not enough; those clean hands, or works, must come from a pure heart.

Simply put, while other books may speak to us, the Word of God has the ability to speak through us.

We must therefore go deeper in our purity. We need to go past the *what* of purity and focus on *why* God calls us to purity and *why* we do what we do. How is this done? Through the Word of God:

> *For the word of God is living and active, sharper than any two-edged sword, piercing to the division of the soul and*

of spirit, of joints and of marrow, and discerning the
thoughts and intentions of the heart.

—Hebrews 4:12

Simply put, while other books may speak to us, the Word of God has the ability to speak *through* us. It is the only book that is supernatural, as it was breathed by God, so it is alive, active, full of energy and power, and able to discern not just the things people do, but also why they do the things they do.

What drives, motivates, and compels you? The Word of God has the power to recognize the outside actions and reveal the inward attitudes.

The Word of God is able to bring us comfort,
joy, peace, love, power, and victory like
nothing else.

My policy, as a pastor of a local church, is to have the Bible on the pulpit lifted high above the congregation; front page and center stage, as that is where the power emanates. I am with John Stott when he declared, "The less the preacher comes between the Word and its hearers, the better."[49] Oh, while I might have some great things to say, teach, and preach based on my experience and education, only God's Word has the supernatural ability to change lives.

And, for the child of God who is walking in the will of God, engaged in the work of God and studying the Word of God, this two-edged sword, or truer to the original language, "surgeon's scalpel," is quite the blessing. Because the Holy Spirit speaks through the Word of God and is able to know our thoughts like no one else, understand what we are feeling like no one else, hear our silent cries like no one else, and see those internal struggles like no one else, the Word of God is able to bring us comfort, peace, joy, love, power, and victory like nothing else.

It is through the Word that we can achieve this depth of purity. That is why a preacher at a men's conference I attended a few years ago kept shouting, "Get your head in the bread!"

So, what then? It should all boil down to:

Our Desire for Purity

Why should we seek purity? What happens to the owner of a pure heart? You "shall see God."

I remember my salvation as if it happened yesterday. Up until that point, I had been sitting in the very back of that church so that I could arrive last and leave first; in and out, just checking church attendance off of my "to do" list. Then something unexpected happened to me:

> Heaven came down and glory filled my soul, when at the cross the Savior made me whole, my sins were washed away and my night was turned to day, Heaven came down and glory filled my soul."[50]

I will never forget leaving that sanctuary that day! As I walked outside, it was as if God had repainted the landscape of the world: trees looked greener, the sky bluer, the sun brighter and my burdens lighter. From that moment on, I could see God!

- I see Him in the gentle breeze on a spring day.

- I see Him in every tree that seems to be reaching up to the sky in praise to the Creator.

- I see Him in the ant crawling on the ground and in the bird flying in the sky.

- I see Him in the bright eyes of a newborn baby.

- I see Him in the lonely gaze held by the wheel-chair-bound senior in the nursing home, looking for Christ and longing for home.

In my life now, everything and everyone I see reminds me of a gloriously powerful and loving God who creates and sustains all life.

Praise God that I can see Him now, but greater still that I will see Him even more clearly later. The apostle Paul speaks of this in terms of seeing God, saying in 1 Corinthians 13:12, "For now we see in a mirror dimly, but then face to face. Now I know in part; then I shall know fully, even as I have been fully known."

One day we will trade in our faith for sight in the lobby of heaven and see God face to face! Oh, what a day that will be! What sight we will have!

Think bigger than the streets of gold, the walls of jasper, the foundation of precious stone, the gates of pearl. Look beyond the friends and family enjoying their new bodies, and the greats and saints from the Bible. Go deeper than the river flowing from God's throne and the Tree of Life, whose leaves are for the healing of the nations, described in chapter 21 of the book of Revelation.

For eternity you will be able to gaze, with a clear focus, into the eyes of the One who set you free and loved you with an everlasting love; you will no longer be tainted by the effects of sin or ravished by age. Finally, for the first time in your life, you will be able to see, really see, your Savior and Father, Jesus Christ. Now *that* is quite the reward for having a pure heart; that is purity worth desiring.

Having a heart that is pure and being rewarded with seeing God is so pleasurable and life-changing that nothing else even compares.

That being said, tragically, there are many times that I have traded that kind of supernatural, heavenly pleasure for the brief, temporal, and hollow pleasures of this world. Remember sixty-two-year-old Mrs. Pennica? According to her "miracle" eye surgeon doctor, surgical techniques available as far back as the 1940s could have corrected her problem. Don't miss this: Mrs. Pennica lived forty of her sixty-two sightless years needlessly blind.

Perhaps you do not have the joy, comfort, and power that come from a pure heart because you have never taken that first step of being poor in spirit. That is the thought brought out in the Christian anthem "Amazing Grace," as the first stanza declares, "I once was lost but now I am found, was blind but now I see."[51]

Please let me introduce you to the Great Physician, who has been performing the same sight-saving procedure for over two thousand years with a one hundred percent success rate. His name is Jesus.

And, once you have Jesus and set your sights on being pure in heart, then you will be able to see God in a more intimate and personal way than ever before.

This is the difference between "seeing is believing" and "believing is seeing." Let me explain. When I was twenty-one years old and searching for answers, I was operating under the "seeing is believing" mentality of the world. I remember being in a hotel room, opening the nightstand drawer and removing a Gideon Bible. I was at the end of my rope, feeling lost, desperate for answers and wanting so badly for God to show Himself, that I might believe.

In fact, I took that Bible out and called out to God, "If you are really there, open this Bible and I will follow you forever." The Bible remained closed. So, I struck another deal. "God," I said, "I will open it for you, just let me open it to a page where it talks about how much you care for me." I forget what page I turned to, but I was still left without my specific request being fulfilled. In a last plea, I asked God to make one of the cars on the highway honk its horn in the next sixty seconds, and that alone would cause me to follow Him. Nothing but silence for the next hour on a highway with heavy traffic.

It was six months later when I called out to Him from my sin and asked Him to be the Lord of my life before I realized the truth: while the world is all about "seeing is believing," faith changes that up with "believing is seeing." Once I came by faith to Him, I saw more clearly than ever before. And in the years since, as I focus on being pure in heart, I have found new aspects of His glory every single day! I have been in a relationship with Him for about thirty years now, and I am still learning about Him and growing in Him.

I hope today that you understand the devotion *to* purity and the depth *of* purity so that you have an insatiable desire *for* purity—to understand that pure is more.

I could not think of a better example of purity than my next friend, Jenn Gotzon Chandler! A model, actress, author, and motivational speaker that radiates with a glow of God's love. I met Jenn a couple of years ago, in the midst of her new adventure, a faith-based movie starring both her and her husband, *The Farmer and the Belle.* Since that day, I have had the privilege of being around her contagious joy that stems from a heart of integrity. Here is what Jenn says about purity:

> Matthew 5:8 says, "Blessed are the pure in heart, for they shall see God." For when our hearts are clouded with chaos, depressive thinking, negative Nancy thoughts, or even bitterness and judgment toward another will create a separation in our mind, body, and then spirit toward our loving living Father. His light for us is real and when we go inward and suffocate under the covers of our own sinful nature, it is hard to see God's goodness. Recognize this and reverse the spiral. Hold each lie captive into the light of Jesus. Hear His voice by praising Him with your heart. In the praise, sing songs and psalms out onto Him and His creation. This will pull the focus to see Him in His fullness and richness of creation. God loves you with an everlasting love that is undeniable. He knocks at our heart and waits for us to open up. When our heart is

closed in misery, our spirit suffers. Focus outward onto His glory, His riches, His providence. See the laughter of a child, hear the wind beneath the wings of the birds as they fly by, see the grass blow in the breeze or the tree leaves flutter to the ground. Now see the life around you. The breath of delight in your spouses' eyes and smile. Life is made by God and His spirit is pure. It is our choice to stay still and mourn or rise up and fight for the new sunrise of each day. It can be very hard but praising Him is your way out of your gloom. Don't stay in the dark. Whisper, "Jesus, Heal me." And He will, miraculously, and then you will see God all around you.

Blessed are the pure in heart, for they shall see God.
—Matthew 5:8

Discussion Questions

1. Have you ever done anything, in a Christian setting, for recognition or reciprocation? Why?

2. What does "seeing God" mean to you personally?

3. In your own words, how can we become pure in heart?

4. How does knowing about your future in heaven affect your living on earth?

To see a video from the author with more thoughts on this topic, and to enjoy more resources, please visit: www.beingthebelieving.com

CHAPTER SEVEN

A Piece of the Peace

Blessed are the peacemakers, for they shall be called sons
of God.
—Matthew 5:9

Of the past 3,400 years, only 268 have found humanity at peace. Twentieth-century wars killed over 100 million people. As many as a billion people have been killed in war throughout human history.[52]

Every year, Christians file millions of lawsuits, including against other Christians.[53] Pastors leave the ministry by the hundreds annually, in part because of interpersonal conflict in their churches. Divorce is as big a problem for Christians as for the general population.

Peace: politicians promise it, beauty pageant contestants propagate it, and world leaders promote it. Humanity has searched for this seemingly elusive, precious commodity since Adam and Eve were dragged, kicking and screaming, from the Garden of Eden.

Yet, for the most part, the church remains silent about these issues, sweeping conflict under the carpet, allowing gossip to spread and looking the other direction at best, or assuming an active role in the conflict at worst.

That is why I am continually urging our church to pray for *unity*! That is why the word "UNITY" is capitalized in our church's name, and why our theme verse is "Behold how good and pleasant it is when brothers dwell in *unity*" (Psalm 133:1, emphasis added).

Why am I so passionate and obsessed about focusing on unity? Because I have seen firsthand what happens where there is no peace: Ichabod, which means "the glory of the Lord has departed", is written on the door to the church, the power of God departs, and we lose our gospel power.

Peace: politicians promise it, beauty pageant contestants propagate it, and world leaders promote it. Humanity has searched for this seemingly elusive, precious commodity since Adam and Eve were dragged, kicking and screaming, from the Garden of Eden.

Even the Antichrist will use the promise of peace to rally the world's politicians, religious leaders, and military to his side during the first three-and-a-half years of the Tribulation period.

The politicians have failed, the beauty pageant contestants have fallen short, and the world leaders—well, turn on your TV!

God still is able to part a sea, tear down a wall, and kill a giant.

The good news is that even though many—and you may be one of them—have been unable to attain peace, peace has come:

> *For to us a child is born, to us a son is given; and the government shall be upon his shoulder, and his name shall be called Wonderful Counselor, Mighty God, Everlasting Father, Prince of Peace.*
> **—Isaiah 9:6**

The Prince of Peace! Praise God, one day Jesus Christ stepped out from eternity in the midst of chaos, turmoil and war and brought peace to a ravished, dry, parched, and weary land.

But knowing that He was about to take on the cross and leave humanity behind, He knew what would happen when His peace departed. He knew that His followers would be discouraged, and that even His closest disciples would start to doubt and question their beliefs.

Why? Because they thought peace was about to leave them. So, before He left, He gave them some comfort:

> *"Peace I leave with you; my peace I give to you,"* said Jesus, *"Not as the world gives do I give to you. Let not your hearts be troubled, neither let them be afraid."*
> —**John 14:27**

Oh, peace is not gone, my friend; it is right here; peace is among us, nay, peace is within us!

That is what makes this next Beatitude so powerful and comforting: "Blessed are the peacemakers, for they shall be called sons of God" (Matthew 5:9).

There are four thoughts I would have us consider as we unpack this verse: *our Christ, our calling, our challenge,* and *our celebration.*

Our Christ as the Example of Peace

Let me preface this point by stating how blessed we are to serve a God who never sets us up for failure by calling us to an impossible task. And He never calls us to do that which He was unwilling to do Himself.

A major part of Jesus' ministry was bringing peace to this world. When He entered into this world, He was hailed as the Prince of Peace, and, more than two thousand years later, peace can still be found wherever the name of Jesus is uttered.

There are several types of peace that Jesus displayed in practical ways:

- *Provisional peace.* In Matthew 14, Jesus brought *provisional peace* to the crowd that was hungry and anxious, not knowing where they would get their next meal. These folks were out in the middle of nowhere, only having five loaves of bread and two fish for five thousand people. This large group discovered that, through Jesus Christ, they were able to realize provisional peace—peace in knowing that God takes care of the needs of His children.

- *Mental peace.* In Mark 5, Jesus brought *mental peace* to the Gerasene maniac, who was possessed with demons, living in a graveyard, torn up in his mind, hailed as crazy by his friends and family, and discarded and forgotten by society. This man was able to realize that, through Jesus Christ, mental peace can bring clarity to a troubled, perplexed, and anxious mind.

- *Practical peace.* In John 2, Jesus brought *practical peace* to the host of a wedding who was stressing because the wine had run dry, leaving them feeling overwhelmed and underqualified to deal with the situation. They were able to realize that, through Jesus Christ, practical peace can overtake the busyness found in everyday life, even when schedules are chaotic, deadlines loom, and tasks look unmanageable.

- *Emotional peace.* In John 4, Jesus brought *emotional peace* to the woman at the well who had a promiscuous past and, I am sure, was unable to look herself in the mirror because of the sinful life she led. She was able to realize that, through Jesus Christ, no matter where she had been or what she had done, emotional peace can cover every sin like a blanket of grace.

- *Physical peace.* In John 8, Jesus brought *physical peace* to the woman caught by the religious leaders of the day, the scribes and the Pharisees, who were about to stone her for the sin of adultery. She was able to realize that, through Jesus Christ, no matter what threats to one's health or safety may be looming in the future, one can enjoy physical peace through a trust that the future is in the hands of a powerful and loving Savior. And, even if physical healing does not come in this life, it is always guaranteed to the child of God in the next.

- *Spiritual peace.* In John 21, Jesus brought *spiritual peace* to Peter. Peter was so close to Jesus that he was offended at the prospect that he would ever deny his Lord. Yet, there came a day when he did just that: he hurt his testimony, compromised with the world, and let down those closest to him. Yet, after the resurrection, his Lord appeared on the shore early in the morning and invited Peter to breakfast. Our Lord chose the morning, when the roosters were crowing, to remind Peter of reconciliation through eternal love. Peter realized that, through Jesus Christ, spiritual peace can come in the midst of failure, in finding a Lord who is longsuffering, patient, kind, and forgiving.

When Jesus Christ died, the veil separating the Holy of Holies from the rest of the temple was torn from top to bottom (Matthew 27:51) and, three days later, the stone was rolled away, revealing an empty tomb from which Jesus Christ emerged in victory (Matthew 28:2–6), demonstrating once and for all that peace is here to stay.

Now that we have established that Jesus Christ has a history of being the peace-giver, we must acknowledge our calling to be peacemakers, or a piece of the peace, by following His examples of peace.

We must realize that our calling involves:

A Heart of Integrity Filled with Peace

It is great that Jesus brought peace to all of those folks in the Bible when He walked the earth more than two thousand years ago, but it is greater still that He brings peace to you and me today. I remember times in my life when I was tossed by circumstance, controlled by emotion, and ruled by my sin. I remember times:

- When, like the Gerasene maniac, I was so caught up in my sin and rebellion that I had no *mental peace*. My mind never shut down; I tossed and turned at night, using alcohol, drugs, toxic relationships, and money to dull it, but I always came up empty until I met Jesus and discovered the mental peace that He offers His children.

- When, like the woman at the well, I was so pulled by this world and tossed by circumstance that I had no *emotional peace*. I was driven by emotion and tossed by circumstance with a life marked with defeat, running in survival mode. I was happy when I had money in the bank and sad when there was none. I was smiling when the sun was shining and frowning when it rained. All week I looked forward to the weekend so that I could dull my senses by yielding to temptation and satisfying the flesh, only to start that cycle all over again on Monday. That was all before I met Jesus and found that He offers emotional peace. And His peace is constant because it is a peace anchored to His unchanging love.

- When, like the adulteress before her accusers, I was so afraid of death itself that I had no *physical peace*. I remember in 1987 being in an accident aboard a ship that left me so injured that I had to be airlifted by helicopter from the middle of the Bering Sea. I thought I was going to die. I fell into depression and was flooded with fear and anxiety.

That was all before I committed myself to Jesus Christ, who has taken away the very sting of death by turning death into the door that ushers us into the presence of our Great Physician. In fact, for the believer, it is only through death that we can ever experience the physical peace that we long for in this fallen world, where our bodies are in a state of decay.

- When, like the host at the wedding, I was feeling so underqualified and overwhelmed by the tasks at hand that I had no *practical peace*. Before Christ, I could not even look anyone in the eyes as I had no self-esteem or confidence, buying into the lie that I was worthless and void of anything valuable. Since I became a follower of Christ, while still overwhelmed and underqualified, I have the confidence that whatever task I may face, obstacle I may encounter, or opponent that may approach, I now know that I can "do all things through Christ who strengthens me" (Philippians 4:13 NKJV). God still is able to part a sea, tear down a wall, and kill a giant. This is called practical peace.

- When, like so many other people, I was so concerned about having more bills than money, that I had no *provisional peace*. I had a habit of staying up late and watching television, especially the "get rich quick" infomercials. In fact, I purchased everything from real estate programs to penny stock investments, all because I was trusting *in* myself to take care *of* myself. Now that I have been adopted into the family of God and am His child, I trust Him to provide for my future; this is a provisional peace that only comes from God.

- When, like Peter, I thought of the many times that I had let my Lord down, hurt those closest to me, and felt lonely, rejected, and tossed aside, even by God Himself, I had no *spiritual peace*. It hurts too much to think of all of the times that I have let my Lord down by my disobedience and sin, yet to know that He will never throw in the towel, wipe His hands, turn His back, and walk away gives me a spiritual peace that only comes from an intimate relationship with Him.

Only Jesus can offer something this world knows nothing about: peace. Jesus Christ came to this dry and thirsty world to bring the kind of lasting peace that only comes from God. He has also brought that peace to our dry and thirsty hearts.

There is no rest in peace in the next life until you claim the Prince of Peace in this life.

Once we have internal peace, we must focus on the external. You cannot bring peace to others until you have experienced peace from within.

This is our calling: we must stand in the midst of humanity and evaluate the culture honestly. Though people may claim that there is peace, we need to acknowledge that there is no peace and encourage people to pursue it through Jesus Christ.

Paul warns, "While people are saying, 'There is peace and security,' then sudden destruction will come upon them as labor pains come upon a pregnant woman, and they will not escape" (1 Thessalonians 5:3).

As children of God, we must not be fooled by a world that declares peace. We must always be honest in our evaluation, recognizing there are many *around* us who do not enjoy the peace that is residing *in* us. Understanding that peace can only come from Christ, not from legislation, prohibition, institution, extrinsic motivation, or intestinal fortitude. Peace comes only from Christ and Christ alone.

An example of this falsely perceived peace is evident when someone dies, especially in Hollywood, in that everyone is quick to put R.I.P. on the gravestone, write it in the paper, post it on social media, and even proclaim it from the pulpit. But we know the truth: there is no rest in peace in the next life until you claim the Prince of Peace in this life, Jesus Christ.

When we become a piece of the peace as Jesus was, we experience:

An Increased Risk for Attempting Peace

If you are the kind of Christian who runs from conflict, buries your head in the sand, simply prays about the dissension in our world, and tolerates disunity, then please hear the words of Jesus in Matthew 10:35–39:

> *For I have come to set a man against his father, and a daughter against her mother, and a daughter-in-law against her mother-in-law. And a person's enemies will be those of his own household. Whoever loves father or mother more than me is not worthy of me, and whoever loves son or daughter more than me is not worthy of me. And whoever does not take his cross and follow me is not worthy of me. Whoever finds his life will lose it, and whoever loses his life for my sake will find it.*

What does all of this mean? It means that when you are a piece of the peace, the peacemaker God has called and empowered you to be, you will be in the very presence of *conflict*.

In fact, you might even *be* that conflict. Christians are dropping out of church, members are fussing and fighting, churches are splitting, ministries are closing, pastors are quitting, and souls are dying and going to hell every single day. We have work to do and peace to bring. That is our calling.

Our Challenge to Show That Example of Peace

Your challenge is simple: be who God has called you to be, in:

Disposition

The first thing Jesus tells us, once we have the truths of the Beatitudes in us, is to be the salt of the earth and the light of the world (Matthew 5:13–16). Oh, the peace that would come into this world if Christians would simply let His light shine before men!

Are you walking around defeated with your head hung low? You are not being a piece of the peace if you look like you've been baptized in pickle juice and are sucking on a lemon. You can't be a piece of the peace if you are going through life with your arms crossed, lips out, with "Bless me if you can" on your swollen tongue. I remember a Christian comedian shouting to a group in church something like, "Don't make me send a missionary to your face!"

Radical lifestyle evangelism is a salve from Satan. It is used by lazy, complacent Christians to soothe the guilt that comes from not being faithful to the Great Commission.

Friend, this world has its fair share of defeated, miserable, and broken people. It's time to show them transformed and renewed lives that shout joy, hope, love, power, and victory. Being a piece of the peace means that because we have been filled with peace from God, we have lives that reflect God. We must have a peaceful disposition. And, we must have peaceful conversation.

Conversation

Our mission is to spread the gospel and make disciples; to reproduce and create other peacemakers. It is way overdue for us to step forward, reach out, and speak up. I dislike the trite saying applied to evangelism, "Spread the gospel and use words if necessary." This is like saying, "Go feed the hungry, and use food if necessary." That is my issue with radical lifestyle evangelism, which is the idea that somehow, just by the lives we live, the lost will be drawn to us like a magnet and transformed by the power of the gospel, without us ever having to say a word.

In my opinion, radical lifestyle evangelism is a salve from Satan. It is used by lazy, complacent Christians to soothe the guilt that comes from not being faithful to the Great Commission. We must not be ashamed of the gospel of Christ. While the lives we live must back up the words we give, we must "preach the Word," being ready "in season and out of season" to "reprove, rebuke, and exhort, with complete patience and teaching" (2 Timothy 4:2). This Beatitude does not say to be peaceful, which is what we enjoy *internally*; it says to be a *peacemaker*, which is what we do *externally*: we make peace.

And, being a piece of the peace requires:

Navigation

We must be proactive. So many believers turn away when there is conflict, shirking their God-given responsibility. This, I believe, is mostly due to fear. Too many Christians have come to believe the loud voices of those who say that Christians are powerless and are not worthy to be heard. The result is that Christians have been silenced and the church has lost its power. Instead, we have been called and empowered to rise up, speak out, and be a piece of the peace, to act on the belief that "greater is he that is in you than he that is in this world" (1 John 4:4 KJV).

Peacemaking means you are proactively looking for opportunities to create a culture conducive to unity.

Years ago, in a church service I was leading, the choir director had everyone seated through a congregational song. This is not unheard of, but the song happened to be "Stand Up, Stand Up for Jesus!" This is what is going on in our world as believers refuse to be the peacemakers God has called them to be while they navigate through this life. There is a big difference between being a peace-keeper and a peacemaker; peacekeeping is more about maintaining the status quo, peacemaking means you are proactively looking for opportunities to create a culture conducive to unity.

Our Celebration for Being That Example of Peace

The reward for being a piece of the peace? We are called sons and daughters of God. This is a title that will usher us into His presence. A title that has changed my very life down here will provide new life up there. What does this title mean? Well, it means several things, actually. The first speaks of:

Nativity Sonship

The very fact that Jesus Christ was born of a virgin means that He was, is, and forever will be known not as "Jesus Christ, son of Joseph" but as "Jesus Christ, Son of God."

And this means that God is now our Father through Christ. You might not have had a great dad on this earth, but you will find no better Father than the One offered in God through His Son, Jesus Christ.

Also, this speaks of:

Covenant Sonship

Jesus Christ lived a sinless life before His Father God and His creation, so that He was able to have a relationship with God that was never severed due to His sin, since He had none.

Because of this, He now offers us the opportunity to share in this covenant sonship with God the Father *through* Him. When we stand before a holy and almighty God, He no longer sees our sin, but His Son, our Savior. So, stop trying to forgive yourself and start enjoying the forgiveness that He has already provided through covenant sonship. The truth is, you are not qualified to forgive yourself; only Christ has that ability. Therefore, through a relationship with God, we not only have forgiveness of our sins but a position as joint heirs of the kingdom of God: covenant sonship.

This also speaks of:

Messianic Sonship

At the cross Jesus cried out: "It is finished!"—meaning He had defeated sin, Satan, and even death (John 19:28–30). He started building His kingdom and will be returning soon.

This world might think it has the upper hand by removing prayer from school, tossing aside the Ten Commandments, and boldly demanding a separation of church and state as they celebrate sin and propagate their wicked agenda through godless organizations like the American Civil Liberties Union and the Freedom from Religion Foundation, celebrating one legal victory after another as they high-five each other behind closed doors.

The devil himself seems to have gotten quite smug and comfortable on this earth, acting like a mouse at play while the cat is away.

Let it be known that Jesus is coming back, not as a lamb led to the slaughter, but as the Lion of the tribe of Judah.

He will come in full pomp and power. Revelation 19:11–16 says:

> *...heaven opened, and behold, a white horse! The one sitting on it is called Faithful and True, and in righteousness he judges and makes war. His eyes are like a flame of fire, and on his head are many diadems, and he has a name written that no one knows except himself. He is clothed in a robe dipped in blood, and the name by which he is called is The Word of God. And the armies of heaven, arrayed in fine linen, white and pure, were following him on white horses. From his mouth comes a sharp sword with which to strike down the nations, and he will rule them with a rod of iron. He will tread the winepress of the fury of the wrath of God the Almighty. On his robe and on his thigh he has a name written, King of kings and Lord of lords.*

And since we are sons of God, we will be right behind Him. In fact, we will have a front row seat to watch Satan, the Anti-Christ, and the false prophet cast into the lake of fire (Revelation 20:10) as we celebrate the end of sin, collectively singing "Victory in Jesus!" for all eternity! That is what Messianic sonship is all about.

Lastly, this title speaks of:

Personal Sonship

Jesus Christ has a personal and intimate relationship

with Father God and—as sons of God—so do we! Never take that for granted. As sons of God, we have audience with the Lord of lords and the King of kings. He actually hears, cares, and is able to move on our behalf. He loves us.

When the church I planted grew to the point that we started using bulletins, I had four Bible verses printed on the bottom of each one, and there to this day they remain: "The sun stood still" (Joshua 10:13); "The iron did swim" (2 Kings 6:6 KJV); "This God is our God" (Psalm 48:14); and "Rejoice in the Lord always" (Philippians 4:4).

I have held many titles through the years: son, petty officer, husband, father, coach, author, professor, politician, and pastor, to name a few. Each of these titles conveys some type of authority, position, or description. Some were earned, others were thrust upon me, but all are from this world. But there is a title that trumps all of these, and that title is son of God. This is a title that was unearned yet is more cherished than any other, for it is not earthly in origin but heavenly, not temporal but eternal. I was asked a few weeks ago what I would want written on my gravestone; I did not have to think on that too long! Oh, how much it would communicate for my tombstone to simply read, "Tom McCracken—son of God"!

Certainly, there are benefits to being called sons of God. But there is only one way that you can be called a son of God, and it's by being a peacemaker.

There is peace available in this world; the question is: will you be a piece of that peace?

Blessed are the peacemakers, for they shall be called sons of God.

—Matthew 5:9

Discussion Questions

1. Have you ever seen or heard of conflict in a church and did not speak up as a peacemaker? Why?

2. In your own words, what is the difference between a peacekeeper and a peacemaker? What makes being a peacemaker more difficult?

3. Should we apply the same principles learned from this chapter to conflict outside of church? Why or why not?

4. What does the possibility of being called a "son of God" mean to you personally?

To see a video from the author with more thoughts on this topic, and enjoy more resources, please visit: www.beingthebelieving.com.

CHAPTER EIGHT

Steps to Victory

Before we move on and unpack the last of the Beatitudes and discover our ultimate reward, let's review what we've learned so far to keep it all in context.

One of the problems facing our culture is that we like to have the best now. We are a self-entitled and instant-gratification-loving society. This is a culture that shuns work, a culture that can be very lazy. Many expect to have everything their grandparents had without going through the sweat, blood, time, and work to have it.

This attitude has crept into the church in the past few years, and so many people think they should have "Peter walking on water" faith the moment they become Christians.

That is why the *health and wealth prosperity* message of today is taking root in our churches. Its message can be summed up by, "Greatness now!": This is verified by the title of a book written by a leader in the prosperity camp, *Your Best Life Now.*[54]

Listen, Christianity is tough. It is hard. It is a journey. It is not instant. Like John MacArthur once said, "If this is your best life now, you are on your way to hell!"[55]

Ever see someone demonstrate great faith through difficult times? I have. In fact, one of the greatest displays of the truth that Christ is enough came from a lady in a nursing home. We will call her Gloria. I had heard through our membership about Gloria, who had been in a terrible car accident in which she lost everything. So, I decided that I would go to that nursing home and visit with Gloria to encourage and pray for her.

When I entered the room, I found a bright-eyed owner of one of those "light up a room" smiles! I thought I had the wrong room. Nope. After a few minutes, I found out that in one tragic car accident she had lost her husband, her legs, her dog, her car, and even her house, as the money from the sale of it was used to pay for her medical bills. Almost in tears after hearing her tragic story, I asked if I could pray for her, to which she replied something like, "I am fine! I still have my Jesus, and He is enough. Let's pray together for all of the hurting and lonely folks in this nursing home." Wow! But that is not even the best part of the story. After I left that room, I went to the nurse's station to ask how long she would be at the facility and to make my intention of future visits known. The nurse told me to check at the information desk before each visit because she was never in the same room. Do you know why? The nursing staff was moving her from room to room to encourage other patients who were discouraged from knee and hip replacement surgeries!

You do not get that kind of faith instantly or without work. That is why I love the Beatitudes. It is here we discover the Christian journey presented in eight steps— eight steps that lead to a victorious, meaningful life, a life full of power because it is a life full of purpose.

Take a step, receive a reward, and move up. Take another, receive a reward, and move up. And by the time you hit the eighth rung of this ladder, you claim victory!

In fact, these Beatitudes have such a progression that when you reach the eighth rung, it is as if you have fought in the Roman coliseum, won the battle, and made your way up the stairs to the Emperor, where you are given a crown of victory—your ultimate reward!

As I stated earlier, these eight steps should be divided into two segments: the first four steps deal with our relationship with God, and the last four deal with the relationships we have with each other.

Our Relationship with God

Step One: Poverty

Blessed are the poor in spirit, for theirs is the kingdom of heaven.
—Matthew 5:3

This does not mean that God blesses those who have no value. Everybody is somebody! For you are created in the image and likeness of God. "The LORD your God is in your midst, a mighty one who will save; he will rejoice over you with gladness; he will quiet you by his love; he will exult over you with loud singing" (Zephaniah 3:17).

Do not believe the devil's lie that you have no value. You are a creation of the living God, and He loves you with an everlasting love.

You will never enjoy a saving relationship *with* God until you *need* a saving relationship *from* God.

To be poor in spirit is to understand that there is nothing you can do to elevate yourself and claim heaven as your future home.

There are no celestial scales that will weigh your good works against your bad ones and *if* the scales tip in your favor, God will allow you entrance into heaven. Those scales simply do not exist.

You can't bring your Bible study, church attendance, money, good deeds, intelligence, baptism, church membership, degrees, or positions held as tickets for admittance into heaven.

So, if we can't be *good enough* to reach heaven, how then are we to obtain a confidence that heaven is our future home?

Rick Warren shook a selfish culture in his book *The Purpose Driven Life* with the revelation that, on earth, it is not about us.[56] Guess what? In heaven it is not about us, either!

Friend, only a humble cry of brokenness will move God's hand of grace in your direction. It is not about what you do or who you are, but what He has done and who He is.

While our goodness can never reach high enough, His grace can reach low enough.

When the appointed time came, God looked down at sinful humanity marked with rebellion and pride and said to His only begotten Son, Jesus Christ, *"I want You to leave glory, don the robes of humanity, be born of a virgin, and become one of them in order to save them all. Suffer, be rejected and despised, and hang on a cross made from a tree that We spoke into existence years ago, suspended halfway between Your home and Your world, with both worlds turning their backs on You as You are left to die. On the third day, You will have the power and authority to raise Yourself from the dead, defeating sin, Satan, and even death itself! You will walk out of that borrowed tomb, demonstrating to an unbelieving world that they can't keep a good Man down!"*

If God believed that your need was so great that He had to sacrifice His only Son, you must also believe that your need is great enough to necessitate that kind of sacrifice.

You will never enjoy a saving relationship *with* God until you *need* a saving relationship *from* God. And when you cry out from that poor spirit, He will give you the kingdom of heaven. Now, that is a reward!

To be taken from the grips of sin and placed in the grips of His grace. To change your father from Satan to Savior. From being controlled by sin to being guided by the Spirit. From hell to heaven, Sinai to Zion, wretched to wealthy, fear to faith, death to life, darkness to light, from "woe is me" to "been set free." That is our reward through salvation!

Step Two: Mourning

> *Blessed are those who mourn, for they shall be comforted.*
> **—Matthew 5:4**

Recently, in one of the small group sessions in our church, a teacher asked the class, "What do the world and the church share in common?" The class was silent, so he then answered for them, "We are all sinners!" Why was the class silent? Because understanding the "why" of the cross makes us uncomfortable since it forces us to admit that we were the ones who caused Jesus Christ to die on the cross.

And, while our *goodness* can never reach high enough, His *grace* can reach low enough.

It always causes me to chuckle whenever I hear someone declare, "I found God," because I know that God was never lost. We are the ones who were lost in the ocean of our sin, but He pursued us. When we send up the Matthew 5:3 beacon of "I am poor in spirit" by confessing that we are spiritually bankrupt and in need of rescue, He pulls us right out of those choppy waves and sets our feet on dry land.

Once you've repented of your sins and are adopted by the King of kings and Lord of lords, you are now a child of God, and your life has been touched by the love of the Master's hand.

You don't have to prove to Him that you love Him by your works, but through your works you seek to please Him as proof of your love for Him.

You now have the best Father a child could ever hope for or dream of. And because of this, you want to show Him that you are thankful that He saved you, changed you, remade you, renamed you, and set you free.

The great news with our Father is that you don't have to *prove* to Him that you love Him by your works, but through your works you seek to *please* Him as proof of your love for Him.

And we do that by mourning, weeping, and grieving over our sin *and* the sins of those around us. Why? Because we know that sin hurts our Father. And for those who have taken that first step, what hurts Him hurts us. We know sin is what caused our Savior to suffer, bleed, and die on the cross, and we don't want Him to suffer any more than He already has. Sin hurts the very heart of the only One who has loved us with an everlasting love.

And what is our reward for caring about our sin so much that we mourn over it? He rewards us with comfort! In sin, we carry around baggage, separation, scars, fear, guilt, shame, and doubt. Yet Jesus Christ tells us that when we mourn over that very sin, He will comfort us.

Step Three: Meekness

Blessed are the meek, for they shall inherit the earth.
—Matthew 5:5

Praise God that when we surrender to the cross, He gives us a power to leave the devil, break free from sin, crucify the flesh, overcome the world, and have hope, joy, love, and the power to walk through this sinful, hurtful, wicked world full of trials, troubles, and tribulation—with joy in our hearts and lives marked with victory.

Now, what do we do with this power in us? We demonstrate meekness, or gentleness. As Kenny Rogers would say, "You got to know when to hold 'em, know when to fold 'em, know when to walk away, and know when to run!"[57]

As children of God, we need to learn when to be gentle and keep our God-given power under wraps and when to give it free rein. When it comes to our feelings, emotions, pride, preferences, visions, dreams, and goals, we should turn the other cheek, let go, and let God.

Have you ever watched the television show *Reba*? In one episode, Reba was stressing about something, and Van said, "I've got one word for you, let it go!" To which

Reba replied, "Van, that is three words." Van said, "Not the way I say it: letitgo!"[58]

You can apply that same concept to walking the Christian walk:

- Church isn't going where you want on a mission trip? Let it go!

- Pastor didn't shake your hand on Sunday? Let it go!

- Don't like the color of the church carpet? Let it go!

- Prefer pews instead of the chairs the church ordered? Let it go!

- Think people should dress up for church instead of wearing jeans? Let it go!

- Prefer contemporary music over traditional hymns? Let it go!

- Want the preaching to last only twenty minutes? Let it go!

While there are times to "let it go," or be gentle, there are also times to be a giant since there are things worth fighting for, such as:

- The helpless widow who is being taken advantage of.

- The lonely husband in the waiting room.

- The abandoned child in the orphanage.

- The person with a disability who is being mocked.

- The doctrines of God's Word.

- The unity within His church.

The key is to know when to be gentle and when to be a giant, or in other words, knowing when to keep our God-given power under wraps and when to give it free rein.

So, what rewards do you get when you take this step and demonstrate meekness? We inherit the earth, both now and then. Or, simply put, power in this life and peace in the next.

Step Four: Hungering and Thirsting

Blessed are those who hunger and thirst for righteousness, for they shall be satisfied.
—Matthew 5:6

Jesus wants His children to get to the point where we have a deep, insatiable, continuous craving for righteousness.

There was a time when I hungered and thirsted after the things of this world—power, popularity, possessions, promotions and prestige—and I was never satisfied. I had a void in my life.

Remember, God created that void. He placed eternity in our hearts (Ecclesiastes 3:11); it is woven into our DNA!

After taking these steps, I can tell you now, with no hesitation, Jesus is enough. I have been made new by the love of God, and now I live each day in awe. I have never gotten over the wonder of it all. I'm completely satisfied with Jesus.

That is why I can be found:

- In church on Sundays and Wednesdays, learning more *about* Him.

- In the hospitals, nursing homes, and funeral homes, telling others *of* Him.

- At church workdays, on the mission field, and in the neighborhoods, serving with others *for* Him.

- At fellowships, banquets, picnics, and gatherings, enjoying others who *love* Him.

I can't get enough of Him. And the reward for that? Satisfaction. We can all enjoy what it means to be full of power in this life and have peace in the next because of a life full of purpose and meaning. That is what Jesus is offering.

In order to be right with God, you can't have left His people!

That brings us to the end of the first four Beatitudes, those that deal with our relationship with God.

In review: as you walked up these steps, submitting to God, though unworthy and undeserving, you were rewarded with the kingdom of heaven, comfort, the inheritance of the earth, and satisfaction in Christ.

These next steps tell you what to do with all that you have been given. In other words, these steps will help you let out what has been let in and be a good steward of the blessings of God.

The tragic reality is that most "Christians" stop after the first four Beatitudes, the *getting* part, and they never move on to the last four, the *giving* part.

And, folks think that they can be right with God but have issues with people. You can't separate your love for God and your love for people; these are married concepts that go hand in hand. In order to be *right* with God, you can't have *left* His people! The apostle John puts it like this: "If anyone says, 'I love God,' and hates his brother, he is a liar; for he who does not love his brother whom he has seen cannot love God whom he has not seen" (1 John 4:20).

So, how do we make sure that we love others? By taking the next steps.

Our Relationships with Each Other

Step Five: Compassion

Blessed are the merciful, for they shall receive mercy.
—Matthew 5:7

I have stated that I like to view the Beatitudes as the ladder that takes us up and closer to God, ultimately bringing us into a victorious Christian life. So, each step follows the previous one, building on each other. This is very evident with this step as we transition from our relationship with God to our relationships with each other.

So, what does mercy mean? What does a life that is compassionate look like? Well, once I realize that I am poor in spirit, I understand there is nothing within me that is righteous, so as a worm I cry out in my lost condition for rescue. And the One who comes to my rescue is a Father who knows me better than everyone else, yet chooses to love me more than anyone else does.

So, I mourn over my sin and the sins of others because I know that sin hurts the very One who loved me enough to rescue me. And, because I know how undeserving I am, I know that I am not better than anyone, just better off. My position in God, through Christ, is tempered with meekness. For I am who I am only by His grace. I know that if anyone knew the real me—where I have been, what I have done, what goes through my mind—I would be alone in this world.

Because I know me as I do and that God loves me anyway, meekness marks my very life. And because God came through the door of my life when everyone else was running out, I have a hunger and a thirst for Him. Why wouldn't I? He is the only one who gave His life so that I could know what living really is.

Therefore, does it not make sense that once I have enjoyed all of the benefits of the love of God, I should view my fellow man in a different light, through the eyes of grace and the lens of His love? That is what being merciful means: to have compassion on other sinners, to look at those outside of His grace with pity and sorrow, knowing they are being held captive by Satan and can't help themselves. This is why Jesus prayed from the cross to His Father, "Father, forgive them, for they know not what they do" (Luke 23:34).

It's bad enough that folks don't love each other in the church, but even more tragic is that this lost world, in desperate need of peace, is looking to the church for answers and walking away empty.

This mercy becomes compassion in action as we reach out with His love to rescue the perishing.

Step Six: Purity

Blessed are the pure in heart, for they shall see God.
—Matthew 5:8

Purity means getting to the point in your life where you have achieved complete clarity and focus on the things of God by banishing evil from your life in order to enjoy the freedoms in Christ that He longs for you to have.

It is simply being honest before God in your evaluation of who you are and who He is, and then allowing God to be God in and through your life.

See God change lives around you because of the love displayed through you by the grace provided in you.

While purity affects your relationship with God, your purity also has an impact on this world. This world is watching you. Your life is a stage. And, they will not be fooled by the Bible carrying, Christian radio playing, Christian flag waving, "Property of God" T-shirt wearing, fish magnet displaying, fair-weather Christian who has become representative of American church culture.

This world is *not* watching you when everything is going well in your life; they only tune in when life gets tough, when things go sideways. For they want to see if what you are wearing, watching, waving, playing and displaying is the real deal; they want to know if you're pure in heart. So, we must show them, like Gloria in the nursing home, that while we are not perfect, we are pure.

The reward for reaching this step and achieving purity in heart? Seeing God! Seeing God means that we are able to:

- Bless those who curse us (Matthew 5:44), because we see that pleasing God is our only goal, not the acceptance of others.

- Go through times of severe trials and suffering because we see that God is able to work all things together for those who love Him (Romans 8:28).

- Reach out to the unreachable and love the unlovable because we see that we can do all things through Christ who gives us strength (Philippians 4:13).

- Cast all of our cares and burdens upon Him because we see that God cares for us (1 Peter 5:7).

- Not worry about tomorrow because we see that God holds tomorrow in His hand.

So, the reward for being pure in heart is to see God change lives *around you* because of the love displayed *through you* by the grace provided *in you*.

Even more tragic is that this lost world, in desperate need of peace, is looking to the church for answers and walking away empty.

Step Seven: Peacemaking

Blessed are the peacemakers, for they shall be called sons of God.
                                        —Matthew 5:9

This culture longs for peace. This world is tired and weary of conflict. They see it between husband and wife, parent and child, employers and employees, brothers and sisters, Republicans and Democrats, and nation and nation.

The church should be the example of peace instead of these statistics:

- Every day, 3,500 people leave the church.[59]

- Four thousand churches close every year.[60]

- Seventy percent of those ages 18 to 22 are dropping out of church.[61]

It's bad enough that folks don't love each other in the church, but even more tragic is that this lost world, in desperate need of peace, is looking to the church for answers and walking away empty.

They look at the church and see the same conflicts they see at home, in politics, at work, on TV, and in their clubs and organizations. And since they walk away not seeing a difference, they walk away unchanged. We are missing the mark.

First Thessalonians 5:14–15 says:

> *And we urge you, brothers, admonish the idle, encourage the fainthearted, help the weak, be patient with them all. See that no one repays anyone evil for evil, but always seek to do good to one another and to everyone.*

D. L. Moody had it right when he declared, "The preaching that this world needs most is the sermons in shoes that are walking with Jesus Christ."[62]

Now that you have completed all seven steps, the eighth step awaits, which is where you find out what reward you get for *Being the Believing*!

Discussion Questions

1. Which of the Beatitudes do you seem to struggle with the most?

2. Why do you think Jesus starts with "Blessed are the poor in spirit"?

3. Which of the Beatitudes is already evident in your life?

4. If you are doing this devotion with someone else or in a group, have everyone share which Beatitude they see as evident in each other's lives. Encourage one another!

To see a video from the author with more thoughts on this topic, and enjoy other resources, please visit: www.be-ingthebelieving.com/videos.

CHAPTER NINE

It Hurts So Good

Blessed are those who are persecuted for righteousness'
sake, for theirs is the kingdom of heaven.
—Matthew 5:10

Imagine in your youth reading of a promised Messiah who would one day come to set the captives free, establish His kingdom, banish the wicked, and rule with a rod of iron through love and power. Imagine you were told of a Messiah who would bring salvation to the lost, comfort to the mourning, restoration of the land to the meek, give satisfaction to the longing, and mercy to the merciful; reveal Himself to the pure in heart; and adopt as His own children those who would strive for peace.

Now, here you are as an adult, sitting at the base of a mountain in the middle of nowhere, looking at this man who claims to be that very Messiah, listening to Him preach, hanging on His every word, hoping beyond hope that now is the time and today is that day.

And He says:

> *Blessed are the poor in spirit, for theirs is the kingdom of heaven. Blessed are those who mourn, for they shall be comforted. Blessed are the meek, for they shall inherit the earth. Blessed are those who hunger and thirst for righteousness, for they shall be satisfied. Blessed are the merciful, for they shall receive mercy. Blessed are the pure in heart, for they shall see God. Blessed are the peacemakers, for they shall be called sons of God.*
>
> **—Matthew 5:2–9**

Imagine your excitement sitting at the base of that mountain as Jesus Christ, the Messiah, preaches through the greatest sermon ever preached, promising great rewards for the demonstration of faith.

Imagine being in that audience—weary and tired of being ruled over by an oppressive government, taken advantage of and mistreated, not to mention being viewed as a stranger in your own Promised Land.

Imagine what these words would mean. They would be life changing. Rewarding. And as if these first seven rewards were not grand enough, He was saving the best for last, as all great teachers do, starting off slow but then building up the momentum, creating an anticipation that intensifies, culminating in an emotional eruption.

So, there you are on cloud nine, excited about this last reward like a child who saved the biggest gift under the tree to open last. Then, Jesus unpacks the last gift in verse 10 by saying, "Blessed are those who are persecuted for righteousness' sake, for theirs is the kingdom of heaven."

You would be shocked! Do all these things and Jesus says your reward is persecution? Heck, you send in $100 to a television evangelist and even he promises you prosperity and puts your name on the TV screen for the whole world to see. This last Beatitude shows that Jesus was not promising that kind of life.

The truth is that if you are not being perse-cuted, you are not Being the Believing!

Jesus knew that this crowd was likely shocked. How do I know that? Well, for seven Beatitudes, Jesus spoke in the third person, using words like "they," "theirs," and "those"; yet after He reveals that the ultimate reward for Being the Believing is persecution, He settles His eternally loving eyes on the crowd and gives an explanation, as well as personalization, with a simple word: "you." If you are not careful, you will miss that subtle shift from third person to second person.

After He knows they are struggling with the idea of persecution, Jesus says, "Blessed are *you.*" He makes it personal and then gives an explanation. There are two reasons why He does this:

First, to reveal that true Christianity is tough, which naturally ushers in an element of anxiety. So, Jesus is revealing that while persecution will come to the Christian, there is a divine purpose; while the first seven Beatitudes are about *character*, this last one is about *confirmation*. When we go to the doctor and have to receive a shot, it is helpful for us to know that the shot is needed and serves a bigger purpose. So, Jesus looks into the eyes of those struggling with the prospect that persecution will come and provides *confirmation* that persecution has a purpose.

And second, to bring *comfort* to those who may be scared, thrown off, anxious, and discouraged that the expectation of the Christian life is to be persecuted. Not only does our Father, the Great Physician, educate His patients that though the shot will hurt, it does have a *purpose,* He makes it *personal* by looking lovingly into their eyes and reminding them that He will be with them through it all, providing comfort and strength.

In our scriptural text, we find that the proof in the pudding for Being the Believing is whether you are being persecuted. And for the most part, Christians in America are not being persecuted. So, either God had it wrong and should have exempted America from this text, or we as Christians in America have it wrong because we are not living the way Jesus said we are to live.

The truth is that if you are not being persecuted, you are not Being the Believing!

Why did Jesus save this Beatitude for last? In the words of R. Kent Hughes, "Its position at the end of the list tells us that it is of supreme importance to the church. Significantly, when stretched on the loom of adversity the church has repeatedly woven persecution and joy into garments of divine praise."[63]

I would add that another reason Jesus saved this for last was to weed out the players, the fence-riders, the noncommittal, and the lukewarm.

Anyone who would step into Christianity after hearing that they would possibly lose their families, homes, jobs, property, and life, is someone who can change this world.

Reviled Because of Your Faith

*Blessed are those who are persecuted for righteousness'
sake, for theirs is the kingdom of heaven.*
—Matthew 5:10

Jesus establishes from the get-go that the reason
Christians will be persecuted is not because of their
personality, bad decisions, past, or sin, but because of the
Savior. This kind of persecution is motivated by two
thoughts:

"For Righteousness' Sake"

First Peter 4:3–4 says:

*For the time that is past suffices for doing what the
Gentiles want to do, living in sensuality, passions,
drunkenness, orgies, drinking parties, and lawless idolatry.
With respect to this they are surprised when you do not
join them in the same flood of debauchery, and they malign
you.*

Like many of you, I had my time with this world and
all of its pleasures, and after tasting all of what the world
had to offer, I was still not satisfied. I still had a void
within me, and I still had no peace. I always walked away
from the things of this world empty, wanting, and
unsatisfied.

Then I met Jesus, and by His grace, I can boldly declare that I have tasted my Lord and found Him to be good, to be enough. I am satisfied.

The time of doing what this world wants is over, and when they hear that I am finished, they do not understand, and they bring persecution.

This world has always persecuted what it does not understand. So, be peculiar, unique, and different, and when—not if, but when—persecution comes, rejoice because you know that persecution means you are doing it right!

For Christ's Account

Persecution has always come to those who have associated with Christ. It's called persecution through proximity. That is why Peter distanced himself from our Lord on the night of His trial and hung out with the heathen instead. He was trying to prove that he was not a disciple of Jesus so he could escape the persecution that comes from associating with Jesus (Luke 22:54–62).

If you do not want to be persecuted, become one with the world. And, if it's any comfort, you will be in the majority, whether you're at home, in the office, or even at church. But, if you are one of the few who long for the day when you can stand before our Father and hear those eternally comforting words, "Well done, good and faithful servant. You have been faithful over a little; I will set you over much. Enter into the joy of your master" (Matthew 25:23), then you will welcome persecution because it is by that very persecution that your life is confirmed, approved, and blessed by God.

A Reaction to Your Faith

Blessed are you when others revile you and persecute you and utter all kinds of evil against you falsely on my account.
—Matthew 5:11

Why will we be persecuted? Because of everything we stand for and all that we believe. Our Founder, whom we love, follow and serve, is the only good in this world. Why does this world hate us to the degree that they cause us to suffer when we are all about goodness?

You will suffer because you are called out. "If you were of the world, the world would love you as its own; but because you are not of the world, but I chose you out of the world, therefore the world hates you" (John 15:19).

Talk about being upfront! If you are a true believer and are living out the seven Beatitudes, you will receive persecution. In a culture where most have intentionally traded persecution for pleasure, this is a shocking concept.

I remember standing outside the front doors of the church after a Sunday service, greeting people, when an older gentleman grabbed my hand and asked with a smile, "How has the world been treating you?"—to which I replied, "The world hates me!" You should have seen the way this man looked at me. He looked at me, perplexed, like a cow looks at a new gate. Next thing I know, he is going to the deacons, requesting prayer for me as he thought I was depressed and in need of intervention!

If you are living for Jesus, expect suffering. Jesus made this fact very clear, for He said, "If the world hates you, you know that it has hated me before it hated you" (John 15:18).

Stand on the rooftops and shout from the highways that Jesus Christ is the only way to salvation, and you will suffer because this world does not know Christ and they will reject any god other than one they can create and manipulate.

You will suffer because you will remove the cloak of sin. "Indeed, all who desire to live a godly life in Christ Jesus will be persecuted" (2 Timothy 3:12).

Though it shouldn't be the only way you share the gospel, as a true believer, you should live in such a way that when you're placed beside an unbeliever or a backslidden Christian, the other person will either get right, get going, or get attacking.

While this is a foreign concept to most American Christians, it was not new to the early church. Next to the unbeliever, the Christian used to stick out like a sore thumb. And again, people persecute that which they do not understand. So, when you refuse to compromise and conform to this world by what you do, where you go, what you watch, and what you wear because of Who you love, suffering will mark your life because you have removed the cloak of sin worn by those around you.

You will suffer because this world does not know Christ. "And they will do these things because they have not known the Father, nor me" (John 16:3).

There are many "religious" people in this world. In fact, according to statistics, more than 90 percent of the world's population believes in something greater than themselves.[64]

While this world may know a religion, this world does not know Christ.

In fact as of a 2010 study, if you consider the major religions of the world—Christianity, Islam, Hinduism, Buddhism, Shintoism, Sikhism, Judaism, Confucianism, Taoism/Daoism, and Jainism—you will find almost six billion adherents to a religion. Amazingly, the world's population in 2013 was only 7.162 billion![65]

Additionally, if you count the indigenous religions, you will soon discover that the true atheists are really the minority. And yet, even with all of these people claiming to believe in something, we are still living in a world full of sin. People are defeated and hopeless and have no peace.

Why? Because while this world may know a religion, this world does not know Christ. Years ago, in North

Carolina, I drove by a church sign that read, "Know God, know peace. No God, no peace." That says it all, for peace only comes from the One born in a manger over two thousand years ago, who was introduced to humanity in Isaiah 9:6 as the "Wonderful Counselor, Mighty God, Everlasting Father, Prince of *Peace*" (emphasis added).

> *If you are Being the Believing, you will suffer because this world is deceived in its concept of God.*

It is not the Muslim, Hindu, Buddhist, Shinto, Sikh, Jewish, Confucian, Taoist, or Jain way. When Jesus stepped out from eternity and introduced Himself to humanity, He boldly declared, "I am the way, the truth and the life. No one comes to the Father but through me" (John 14:6). And, by that statement alone, He offends every tribe, tongue, kindred, nation, and people group that claims there are other ways to heaven.

You want to see persecution? Tell the 1.8 billion Muslims who worship Allah that they are on the path to hell. [66]

Tell the 1.1 billion Hindus, who worship 330 million gods and goddesses, that their worship is in vain.[67]

Tell the Buddhists that their founder, Siddhartha Gautama, was deceived by a demon and their prayers are not being heard.

Stand on the rooftops and shout from the highways that Jesus Christ is the only way to salvation, and you will suffer because this world does not know Christ and they will *reject* any god outside of the one they can create and manipulate. In contrast, they will *receive* any god that will not judge their sin or seek to change how they live and who they want to be.

You will suffer because this world is deceived in its concept of God. John 16:1–4 says:

> I have said all these things to you to keep you from falling away. They will put you out of the synagogues. Indeed, the hour is coming when whoever kills you will think he is offering service to God. And they will do these things because they have not known the Father, nor me. But I have said these things to you, that when their hour comes you may remember that I told them to you.

If you are Being the Believing, you will suffer because this world is deceived in its concept of God.

This world has no issues with certain attributes of God or segments of the Bible. In fact, most love to hear that God is an ever-present help in time of trouble (Psalm 46:1) and that He will protect, provide for, give strength to, and unconditionally love all people.

Their perverted view is that God has created a world of roses and we are all His children, holding hands and singing "Kumbaya" as we enjoy His love all the way to heaven. But things get ugly and persecution comes when you start to talk about His holiness, wrath, anger, hatred of sin, accountability, and His call to repentance.

Our Suffering Is for a Purpose

Suffering for Christ brings us closer *to* Him, makes us more *like* Him, and reminds us that we are *of* Him. Luther once said, "I am getting rather proud, for I see that my character is more and more defamed."[68]

When we are Being the Believing, we will suffer persecution and can be confident that this suffering has a purpose.

In 2015, I ran a successful campaign for a seat on the school board. During this campaign, in which I experienced persecution for my faith, someone wrote an editorial and submitted it to the local paper in support of my election. One of the deacons of our church viewed some of the comments in response to that editorial and was concerned that I would be upset by some of the negative remarks against me, which ranged from calling me a "religious nut" to likening me to a member of ISIS!

But I was far from upset. In fact, I rejoiced! Why? Because when we are Being the Believing, we will suffer *persecution* and can be confident that this suffering has a *purpose*.

Our Suffering Is Not Permanent

There is coming a day when those clouds will be rolled

back like a scroll, the trump shall resound, and our Lord shall descend. A day when my Jesus will show all of those faith healers how it's really done by whisking the Holy Spirit down every hallway of every nursing home and hospital, past every room where born-again believers are hurting and lonely, longing for relief and peace, and He will give them a new body that will have no need for medications, visitations, or lamentations. This present existence has a very short shelf-life!

When my oldest daughter, while serving in the United States Air Force, was at technical school in Texas for three months, she discovered she was the only virgin in her flight. She was the only one who went to church every Sunday and the only one who said "no" when literally everyone else around her enjoyed the things of the world. As a result, there were times that she felt lonely and became tired of being isolated, often being alone on the weekends.

For those like my daughter, living for Christ and facing the promised persecution, there is comfort in the knowledge that our suffering is not permanent. For there is coming a day, and it will be soon, when we will either come into His presence through the casket or the clouds, and will realize when we trade in our faith for sight at the gates of glory and look around, that it was worth it all. As Tony Campolo declares, "It's Friday, but Sunday's comin'!"[69]

Rewarded for Your Faith

*...for your reward is great in heaven, for so they persecuted
the prophets who were before you.*
—Matthew 5:12b

This audience of early believers never experienced the
rewards American Christian culture has been propagating,
presenting, and proclaiming in the prosperity message of
today: get saved, get rich, get healthy, get popular, get
powerful, and get successful. Of course, that message is
usually followed up with how much seed money you will
need to mail in.

Those are *not* the rewards that God has promised to
those who place their faith and trust in Him. While He is
a "rewarder of those who diligently seek Him" (Hebrews
11:6 NKJV), it is imperative that we *define* the reward that
God grants to those who demonstrate faith.

The Bible is not silent on this issue; in fact, the entire
eleventh chapter of Hebrews is given to demonstrate what
faith is, some examples of who had it, how we can get it,
and what it does. These "people of old"—Abel, Enoch,
Noah, Abraham, Sarah, Isaac, Jacob, Joseph, Moses,
Joshua, and Rahab—never ate what the proponents of the
prosperity message dish out, but they were rewarded.
Their reward for faith? The approval of God.

That's it. The confidence, assurance, and blessing of
knowing that you are right with God, that when you take
the steps that He has approved, you will be protected, provided for, and the recipient of His promises.

Being able to lie down at night and know that whatever tomorrow holds, you know Who holds tomorrow is a far better reward than good health, lots of money, a stable job, and a nice house.

I'll take a great God in glory over any good thing on earth any moment of any day. It has worked for three decades, and I am not about to trade down now!

Rewards Build Faith

Simply put, when God rewards our faith, our faith grows. Because God has demonstrated His ability in our past, we can be confident of His authority in our present and celebrate what we will achieve in the future!

When Abraham, the father of the nation of Israel, stepped out from the comfort and security of his own land to venture out into the unknown (Genesis 12), he saw the hand of God move and he was rewarded. By the time he was asked to offer his only son, Isaac (Genesis 22), he had a past with God and his faith in Him was built up so much that he gladly spoke up, stepped out, and surrendered to His will.

Most of us have a past with God. I have a past with God, filled with His power, and motivated by His love. Let me share a little about what God has done in our family. In 1994, after years of seeing infertility specialists and suffering through a miscarriage, my wife became pregnant again. She was classified as high risk, placed on all kinds of supplements, and remained under the watchful eye of our doctor.

About three months into the pregnancy, my wife was walking down the hallway of our home in North Carolina when she dropped to the floor on her knees in pain and cried out that something was wrong. I hit the living room floor and cried out to God in prayer. Afterward, the doctors could find nothing wrong, and a few months later, our daughter was born healthy. This is the daughter I talked about earlier, who served in the Air Force.

Because God has demonstrated His ability in our past, we can be confident of His authority in our present and celebrate what we can achieve in the future.

Two years later, in 1996, my wife got pregnant again. This time, the nine months were rather uneventful, but the labor was drawn out and hard. When our middle daughter was delivered, she was paralyzed on one side of her face due to the use of forceps, as she had been born breech. The doctors did not know if this would be permanent or temporary, so we prayed. God healed her, and she is now the most beautiful young lady, who also served our county in the United States Air Force.

Then three years later, in 1999, we had a surprise when my wife became pregnant again. During a routine ultrasound, at about three months, the expression on the nurse's face concerned us, and when she dismissed herself, mid-test, to go get a doctor, we knew that something was wrong. That day ended in a conference room with our doctor, nurse, and a counselor as they informed us that the ultrasound revealed that our child would be born with spina bifida and that the collective recommendation was to terminate the pregnancy.

Well, by that time in our lives, after all that we had been through with our other children, we just looked at that group of "experts" and basically said, "You all better buckle up because our God is about to show up!" And show up He did! Our youngest daughter is healthy and beautiful, currently serving her country in the United States Navy. Again, because God has demonstrated His ability in our *past*, we can be confident of His authority in our *present* and celebrate what we can achieve in the *future*.

Now, I am not saying that God always chooses to fix everything that is broken down here. Remember the list of my current ailments? What I am saying is that we can trust Him based on the history He has with us. Even if you just look to the past, looking no further than what He did on the cross, we can move forward with the confidence that He will provide in the future.

I have a past with the Almighty God, so I have no problem believing that God will work everything out in the end and that He will reward me one day as His child!

Final Thoughts

Well, this has been quite the journey. We have been poor, mourned, displayed meekness, hungered and thirsted after the things of God, displayed mercy, shunned hypocrisy, and brought peace to a chaotic world, with our ultimate reward of being persecuted—causing us to run around the room, hands in the air, skipping and jumping for joy as if we had won the lottery!

How? Because:

1. Your reward in heaven is great!

James says, "Blessed is the man who remains steadfast under trial, for when he has stood the test he will receive the crown of life, which God has promised to those who love him" (James 1:12). We will receive crowns!

And Revelation gives us a clear picture of what we will be doing with our crowns, or rewards, in heaven: "…the twenty-four elders fall down before him who is seated on the throne and worship him who lives forever and ever. They cast their crowns before the throne" (Revelation 4:10).

I remember as a child being invited to a birthday party by a friend. My friend told me at school that no presents were required, just to come over and watch movies and play games. Well, there I stood that night in his living room as he opened presents from everyone else who came. I felt like a heel, like I didn't even deserve to be his friend or attend his party. I never want to feel that way again. You see, the rewards that Jesus is speaking of are not for our glory but for His! And we can live our lives in such a way down here that we don't have to feel like a heel one day up there.

2. This world has no claim on your reward!

I can't think of a better story to make this point than that of John Chrysostom:

> Chrysostom was "a godly leader in the fourth-century church, who preached so strongly against sin that he offended the unscrupulous Empress Eudoxia as well as many church officials.
>
> When summoned before Emperor Arcadius, Chrysostom was threatened with banishment if he did not cease his uncompromising preaching.
>
> His response was, "Sire, you cannot banish me, for the world is my Father's house."
>
> "Then I will slay you," Arcadius said.
>
> "Nay, but you cannot, for my life is hid with Christ in God," came the answer.
>
> "Your treasures will be confiscated," was the next threat, to which John replied, "Sire, that cannot be, either. My treasures are in heaven, where none can break through and steal."
>
> "Then I will drive you from man, and you will have no friends left!" was the final, desperate warning.
>
> "That you cannot do, either," answered John, "for I have a Friend in heaven who has said, 'I will never leave you or forsake you.'"
>
> John was indeed banished, first to Armenia and then farther away to Pityus on the Black Sea, to which he never arrived because he died on the way. But neither the banishment nor his death disproved or diminished his claims. The things that he valued most highly not even an emperor could take from him."[70]

And it is not enough that we are persecuted, for that comes externally and quite often; it is out of our control. What is in our control is the attitude with which we address that persecution. Hebrews 10:34 gives us insight as to the proper attitude: "For you had compassion on those in prison, and you *joyfully accepted* the plundering of your property, since you knew that you yourselves had a *better possession* and an abiding one" (Hebrews 10:34, emphasis added).

Use that persecution as a stage on which to communicate to this world that Jesus Christ is enough.

Joyfully accepted the plundering of their property! What? We freak out when Dish Network drops the Fox channel and when the cost of stamps increases by two cents! Our world is turned upside down when we lose a job, our health, or a loved one. These folks joyfully accepted being dragged out of their homes, losing their jobs, being separated from their families, and even facing the prospect of a painful death by torture. Joyfully accepted! They didn't merely tolerate or put up with it; they accepted radical persecution with joy. While the persecution was radical, so was their joyful response. That is how they were able to change the world; they were Being the Believing.

How could they joyfully accept all of the trials that came into their lives? Because they knew they had a better possession. Matthew 13:44 reads, "The kingdom of heaven is like treasure hidden in a field, which a man found and covered up. Then in his *joy* he goes and sells all that he has and buys that field" (emphasis added). This man found something valuable, and so he went and sold all that he had and purchased a field that, in the eyes of the world, seemed to be a waste of money. Folks treated him as crazy, but he was able to smile because he knew he had a better possession!

The world may not want to see and understand our better possession in Christ. The cross may be foolishness to them because they refuse to taste and see that the Lord is good. But we have seen and understood what we have in Christ. The cross is not foolishness to us but rather the door by which we have access to God, our sure and steadfast anchor of the soul. Since we have tasted and we have found the Lord to be good, we can accept any trial, trouble, or tribulation with joy in our hearts, a spring in our step, and our head held high—because we have a better possession, and an abiding one, in the salvation of our Lord!

If you are Being the Believing, persecution will come; the key is to use that persecution as a stage on which to communicate to this world that Jesus Christ is enough.

Discussion Questions

1. Have you ever been persecuted for your evident and outward love for Christ? Explain.

2. What does the author mean when he states that we can use persecution as a stage on which to present Jesus Christ as sufficient and enough?

3. Who is your favorite person in the Bible, and what is your favorite account about how they used persecution to showcase the sufficiency of God? Explain.

4. The title of this chapter is "It Hurts So Good." Have you ever experienced this? Explain.

To see a video from the author with more thoughts on this topic, and to enjoy other resources, please visit: www.beingthebelieving.com.

CHAPTER TEN

Start Being the Believing
with Dr. Fredric Eichelman

Being the Believing is so much more than walking down the aisle of a church, making an emotional plea, being baptized, having your name written on the membership roll, singing in the choir, teaching a small group class, or even preaching a sermon. It is all about a transformation in your life from a confrontation with the resurrected Son of God, Jesus Christ. Being the Believing is the difference between *doing good* and *being good*.

I hope you have discovered the joy that comes from giving up on doing good and allowing God to fill you with good. And, I hope that Being the Believing marks your life as you show this world, by your works, that you now have God's power within you.

I want to share a true story as related by Dr. George Pentecost:

A distinguished Christian lady was recently spending a few weeks at a hotel at Long Branch, and an attempt was made to induce her to attend a dance, in order that the affair might have prestige bestowed by her presence, as she stood high in society. She declined all the importunities of her friends, and finally an honorable senator tried to persuade her to attend, saying, "Miss B., this is quite a harmless affair, and we want to have the exceptional honor of your presence." "Senator," said the lady, "I cannot do it. I am a Christian. I never do anything during my summer vacation, or wherever I go, that will injure the influence I have over the girls of my Sunday School class." The senator bowed, and said, "I honor you; if there were more Christians like you, more men like myself would become Christians."[71]

When hard times come, tears are shed, and hearts are hurting, know this; there is no hurt on earth that heaven cannot heal!

Being the Believing is all about advancing through the Beatitudinal ladder. It is a life that enjoys the benefits of being a child of the King, and of being so excited and passionate about those benefits that you can't wait to share this blessed state with others. Being the Believing means that we have:

Access to the Throne of God

There was a time when people trembled at the *power* of God and hid from the *presence* of God. Terrifying was His power and presence on that holy mountain, lit up with lightning and booming with thunder (Exodus 20:18). The average person dared not approach the mountain of God or enter into the Holy of Holies, lest they receive the full brunt of the wrath of God. That was all before Jesus came to fulfill the law and take us from a dispensation of law to the dispensation of grace.

Hebrews 12:22 says, "But you have come to Mount Zion and to the city of the living God, the heavenly Jerusalem." Mountains will fade, tabernacles and temples will crumble, and even our precious church buildings will be destroyed because they are all temporary, but our relationship with God is not material or external; rather, it is spiritual and internal. We can walk, talk, fellowship, and worship with God anywhere and at any time. This world can't touch the eternal, and circumstance doesn't have to affect the internal. There are so many "Christians" who are not living out this belief. They might sing "Power in the Blood" on Sunday and even throw out an "Amen" or two when they hear these truths, but the moment they get some bad news from the doctor, an unexpected phone call, or that unexpected bill in the mailbox, their worlds are flipped upside down and defeat marks their very lives.

When hard times come, tears are shed, and hearts are hurting, know this; there is no hurt on earth that heaven cannot heal. As children of God we can, according to Hebrews 4:16, boldly enter into His throne room of grace.

Oh, the joy to know that whatever the time, wherever the place, whoever the seeker, that the living, fearful, terrible, awesome, mighty, powerful God is giving us the invitation to come to His mountain, sit on His furniture, and enter into His presence without fear of wrath but to experience His love, mercy, and grace. Being the Believing means that as we navigate through this life full of trials, tribulations, and troubles, we can have a confidence and assurance that comes from the knowledge that our God has filled us with power and given us a purpose.

But there is coming a day when we will take those glimpses of glory for an extended journey into forever!

And Being the Believing means that we have a better future!

Adoration with the Throng Before God

While we have church services down here that are powerful and engaging, glimpses of glory where the power and presence of Christ is felt, they will remain just glimpses until we leave this world. But there is coming a day when we will take those glimpses of glory for an extended journey into forever! (see Revelation 7:11). As the old hymn proclaims,

> What a day that will be, when my Jesus I shall see—when I look upon His face, the One who saved me by His grace. When He takes me by the hand and leads me through the Promised Land, what a day, glorious day, that will be![72]

Being the Believing means that no matter our lot in this life, we will be trading up in the next.

And Being the Believing means that when life is over and eternity is about to start, we will have:

Acceptance in the Court of God

I had a bad experience in 1988 when I was pulled over by a young, cocky, and angry state police officer, who was confronted with a young, cocky, and angry Tom. He won because he had a gun. He handcuffed me, threw me in the back of his car, drove me to the station, and left me hand-cuffed in a cell, and there I waited. I was scared and anxious and did not want to stand before a judge in a court of law, for I was guilty. To this day, whenever I hear a siren or see those blue and red lights flashing, I am that young man in the cell, scared all over again.

Oh, friend, let me tell you the good news today! One day, we will stand before the Judge of all, and because of what Jesus Christ has done, we will not have to plead guilty, not guilty, or insanity, but simply plead the name of Jesus (see Revelation 14:13). Nothing to the throne I bring; simply to the cross I cling!

Being the Believing is a life that speaks of an under-standing that the only One we need to please can be pleased by Being the Believing.

Before we come to the end of this journey, I want to introduce you to another friend of mine, Dr. Fredric Eichelman. I have the privilege of holding the title of Dr. Eichelman's pastor, a title I do not take lightly. I can't think of a better story that reveals a life that has moved up

the Beatitudinal ladder than Dr. Eichelman's. An educator
in the public school system for over forty years, he has
had his ups and downs, yet he remains a constant force of
faith that is Being the Believing. Here, he describes that
journey in his own words:

I made the decision to be a teacher when I was in
high school, though I also had a dream since childhood of being an author. During my senior year in
college, I applied to teach in several school systems
and was especially interested in Roanoke County
Schools in my home state of Virginia.

When I met with the superintendent, he made a
comment that changed my plans. "We need more
male administrators in our elementary schools and
your serving as editor of your college newspaper
reveals you would do better to be a school principal."

That was a heady thing to hear, so I studied for a
master's degree to go into administration. After
teaching four years in upper elementary grades, the
superintendent was true to his word. I was appointed to be a principal of an elementary school,
one located in Salem. Though I missed teaching, I
adjusted easily to being the youngest principal in
the school system. On top of that, I was privileged to
help make plans for building an exciting new elementary school that would replace the building I
was in. Some would say I was in the fast lane to better things.

The new school was built, and we were set for the
dedication when a funny thing happened on the
way to the new building's first PTA meeting. My
brakes failed at a railway crossing, and a passing

train hit my car. I was lucky I survived with only a badly broken hip; however, in the hospital, I got bad news. The county administration feared that a principal using a walker, later a cane, would not be respected by students and not able to discipline. So, this "in the fast lane guy" was derailed and wound up in the school board office for a few years on numerous projects.

However, something even better happened. My church activities increased, and I read and studied a great deal more about the Christian faith. Though a Christian since a kid, I had been more of an observer than an active member. I started teaching Sunday school, and that gave me an opportunity to use good films and books to reach students.

Finally, after a while, I got back to where I originally planned to be, which was teaching in a high school, where I remained for twenty-one years, getting my doctorate and becoming the head of the social studies department. It was in that position that led me to be active in working with media and other conventions, writing textbooks, and even having a major involvement in politics.

Teaching and writing had been my dream as a kid, and I had lost that dream until God got ahold of my life and things changed big time. Though I am now in my eighties, God is still guiding my life.

Closing Challenge

In the 1991 movie *Hook*, Robin Williams plays the grown-up Peter Pan, who has returned to Neverland and finds himself trying to prove, to the still-young Lost Boys, that he is, in fact, Peter Pan.[73] The Lost Boys are unable to recognize Peter as he has grown old, gained weight, is wearing glasses, and has wrinkles. Tinker Bell, who knows this aged man to be the real Peter Pan, convinces some of the Lost Boys to give Peter a second look.

After everyone has given up, the smallest of the Lost Boys makes his way over to Peter, guides him down to his knees, so that he can look at him face to face, and gives Peter a closer look. He removes Peter's glasses, and with both hands, pushes back the wrinkles on his forehead, straightens out the wrinkles around his eyes, and then pushes the wrinkles on his cheeks far out of the way to remove the many years. While holding the wrinkles back, he looks into Peter's eyes and declares, "Oh, there you are Peter!"—a revelation that causes many of the cynical and unbelieving Lost Boys to rush over with joy and become filled again with hope.

I believe this to be the problem with the bride of Christ today. We have allowed complacency to fatten the church, selfishness to add many wrinkles, and organization, legalism, and politics to dull her vision. Meanwhile, the world around us still hears and sees us but is unable to recognize the once purpose-driven organism that had the power to change the world. I am convinced that once we start Being the Believing, the lost people in this world will give us a closer look, push back our wrinkles, dysfunction, and sin, and declare, "Oh, there you are, Church!"

What would happen to the world *around* us if the One *within* us could be seen free from distractions, distortions, and dysfunction? What if the church could really be *seen* by this world? What if you would declare today, "I am Being the Believing?" What if?

Discussion Questions

1. What part of this book resonated the most in your life?

2. What specific changes do you need to make before you can declare, "I am Being the Believing"?

3. Who can be your accountability partner as you affect the needed changes in your life? And, who will you decide to pray for and help as they become part of Being the Believing?

About the Author

Tom McCracken is a church planter, professor, and a gifted communicator who has been highlighted on national television for his innovative methods of spreading the gospel. He has earned degrees in business and theology, holds a post graduate degree in education (Ed.S), and is currently a doctoral candidate in education, working on his dissertation through Liberty University in Lynchburg, Virginia. Tom would love to hear how this book has impacted your life! Please visit www.beingthebelieving.com for contact information and to inquire about booking Tom to speak to your church or group.

About SermonToBook.Com

SermonToBook.com began with a simple belief: that sermons should be touching lives, *not* collecting dust. That's why we turn sermons into high-quality books that are accessible to people all over the globe.

Turning your sermon or sermon series into a book exposes more people to God's Word, better equips you for counseling, adds credibility to your ministry, and even helps make ends meet during tight times.

John 21:25 tells us that the world itself couldn't contain the books that would be written about the work of Jesus Christ. Our mission is to try anyway. Because, in heaven, there will no longer be a need for sermons or books. Our time is now.

If God so leads you, we'd love to work with you on your sermon or sermon series.

Visit www.sermontobook.com to learn more.

REFERENCES

Notes

[1] Lewis, C. S. *Mere Christianity*. MacMillan Publishing Company, 1952, p. 54–56.

[2] Strong, James. "Strong's Greek #1491: Eido." In *A Concise Dictionary of the Words in the Greek Testament and the Hebrew Bible.* Faithlife, 2019.

[3] "Lists: All Countries." The Joshua Project. Frontier Ventures. 2019. https://joshuaproject.net/global/countries.

[4] Pritchard, Ray. "The Making of a Disciple." Keep Believing. January 7, 1996. https://www.keepbelieving.com/sermon/the-making-of-a-disciple/.

[5] Hughes, R. Kent. *The Sermon on the Mount: The Message of the Kingdom.* Crossway, 2013.

[6] Strong, James. "Strong's Greek #4434: ptochos." In *A Concise Dictionary of the Words in the Greek Testament and the Hebrew Bible.* Faithlife, 2019.

[7] Toplady, Augustus M. "Rock of Ages." 1776. In Hymnary.org. https://hymnary.org/text/rock_of_ages_cleft_for_me_let_me_hide.

[8] Watts, Isaac. "Alas, And Did My Savior Bleed." 1707. In "Hymn Text Comparison: Alas, And Did My Savior Bleed," Hymnary.org. https://hymnary.org/text/alas_and_did_my_savior_bleed/compare#.

[9] Carey, William. In "Pages from History: William Carey Passes Away (1834)." Nalloor Library. June 4, 2014. https://nalloorlibrary.com/tag/william-carey/.

[10] Rainer, Thom. "Hope for Dying Churches." Facts & Trends. Lifeway. January 16, 2018. https://factsandtrends.net/2018/01/16/hope-for-dying-churches/.

[11] Smith, Oswald J. *The Man God Uses.* Marshall, Morgan & Scott, 1943, p. 18.

[12] Lowry, Mark. "Mark Lowry—A Message from Mark—Recovering Fundamentalist." YouTube. July 22, 2016. https://www.youtube.com/watch?v=z2aeDPsrAaQ.

[13] Bartlett, E. M. "Victory in Jesus." 1939. In Hymnary.org. https://hymnary.org/text/i_heard_an_old_old_story_how_a_savior.

[14] Strong, James. "Strong's Greek #3076: Lypeite." In *A Concise Dictionary of the Words in the Greek Testament and the Hebrew Bible.* Faithlife, 2019.

[15] House, Paul R. "Introduction to Jeremiah." *ESV Study Bible.* Crossway, 2008, p. 1364.

[16] Page, Frank S. "The Sower and the Soils." *SBC Life.* September 1, 2014. http://www.sbclife.net/article/2304/the-sower-and-the-soils.

[17] Autry, Brian. Speech at Southern Baptist Conservatives of Virginia Pastor Luncheon, Green Ridge Baptist Church, Roanoke, Virginia, August 2015.

[18] Colson, Charles. *Who Speaks For God?* Tyndale House, 1994.

[19] "Our Story." The Work of a Carpenter Ministries. https://www.theworkofacarpenterministries.org/our-story.

[20] Hecht, Mindy. "The 613 Commandments (Mitzvot)." In Chabad.org. https://www.chabad.org/library/article_cdo/aid/756399/jewish/The-613-Commandments-Mitzvot.htm.

[21] MacArthur, John. *The Only Way to Happiness: The Beatitudes.* Moody Publishers, 1998, p. 99.

[22] Sherman, Richard B. and Richard M. Sherman. "A Spoonful of Sugar." *Mary Poppins (Original Soundtrack).* Walt Disney Records, 1964.

[23] Forest, Jim and James H. Forest. *The Ladder of the Beatitudes.* Orbis Books, 1999.

[24] McGraw, Phillip. *Philisms.* Simon & Shuster, 2003.

[25] Piper, John. "God Is Most Glorified in Us When We Are Most Satisfied in Him." Desiring God. October 13, 2012. https://www.desiringgod.org/messages/god-is-most-glorified-in-us-when-we-are-most-satisfied-in-him.

[26] Strong, James. "Strong's Greek #1556: Galal." In *A Concise Dictionary of the Words in the Greek Testament and the Hebrew Bible.* Faithlife, 2019.

[27] Moody, Josh. "This Day in History: Jonathan Edwards Preaches 'Sinners in the Hands of an Angry God.'" Crossway. July 8, 2018. https://www.crossway.org/articles/this-day-in-history-jonathan-edwards-preaches-sinners-in-the-hands-of-an-angry-god/.

[28] Spafford, Horatio Gates. "When Peace Like a River Attendeth My Way." 1873. In Hymnary.org. https://hymnary.org/text/when_peace_like_a_river_attendeth_my_way.

[29] "Sanctification." In *Baker's Evangelical Dictionary of Biblical Theology.* Edited by Walter A. Elwell. Baker Books, 1996. In Bible Study Tools. https://www.biblestudytools.com/dictionary/sanctification/.

[30] Ward, Mark, Sr. The Lord's Radio: Gospel Music Broadcasting and the Making of Evangelical Culture, 1920–1960. McFarland, 2017, p. 173.

[31] "Muhammad." Biography. November 5, 2019. https://www.biography.com/religious-figure/muhammad.

[32] Ayoub, Mamoud. *A Muslim View on Christianity: Essays on Dialogue.* Orbis Books, 2007.

[33] La Vey, Anton. *The Satanic Bible.* Harper Collins, 1976.

[34] "Bureau of Labor Statistics 2016 Consumer Expenditure Survey." BLS Reports. Bureau of Labor Statistics. April 2018. https://www.bls.gov/opub/reports/consumer-expenditures/2016/home.htm.

[35] Piper, John. "Why I Abominate the Prosperity Gospel." Desiring God. October 29, 2008. http://www.desiringgod.org/interviews/why-i-abominate-the-prosperity-gospel.

[36] MacArthur, John. *The MacArthur New Testament Commentary.* Moody Publishers, 2011.

[37] MacArthur, *MacArthur New Testament Commentary.*

[38] Cook, Philip W. "Appendix." In *Abused Men: The Hidden Side of Domestic Violence.* 2nd ed. Praeger, 2009, p. 198.

[39] Patchin, Justin W. "Millions of Students Skip School Each Year Because of Bullying." Cyberbullying Research Center. January 3, 2017. https://cyberbullying.org/millions-students-skip-school-year-bullying.

[40] O'Donnell, Douglas Sean. *Matthew: All Authority in Heaven and on Earth.* In *Preaching the Word*, edited by R. Kent Hughes. Crossway, 2013.

[41] MacArthur, John. *Matthew 1–7.* In *The MacArthur New Testament Commentary.* Moody, 1985.

[42] "Pity." *Lexico.* https://www.lexico.com/en/definition/pity.

[43] Saint Augustine. Quoted in John MacArthur, *The Only Way to Happiness: The Beatitudes* (Moody, 1998), p. 143.

[44] MacArthur, *Matthew 1–7*, p. 196.

[45] Ten Boom, Corrie. "I'm Still Learning to Forgive." In *Guideposts*, 1972. Quoted in "Guidepost Classics: Corrie ten Boom on Forgiveness," July 24, 2014. https://www.guideposts.org/better-living/positive-living/guideposts-classics-corrie-ten-boom-on-forgiveness.

[46] Hughes, R. Kent. *The Sermon on the Mount: The Message of the Kingdom.* In *Preaching the Word*, edited by R. Kent Hughes. Crossway, 2013.

[47] Fackler, Mark. "The World Has Yet to See…" Christianity Today. https://www.christianitytoday.com/history/issues/issue-25/world-has-yet-to-see.html.

[48] Godlaski, Theodore M. "Shiva, Lord of Bhang." *Substance Use & Misuse.* 47, no. 10 (2012): p. 1067–1072. DOI: 10.3109/10826084.2012.684308.

[49] Stott, John R. W. *The Preacher's Portrait.* Wm. B. Eerdman's Publishing, 1961, p. 30.

[50] Peterson, John Willard. "Heaven Came Down." 1961. In Hymnary.org. https://hymnary.org/text/o_what_a_wonderful_wonderful_day.

[51] Newton, John. "Amazing Grace! (How Sweet the Sound)." 1779. In Hymnary.org. https://hymnary.org/text/amazing_grace_how_sweet_the_sound.

[52] Hedges, Chris. "What Every Person Should Know About War: First Chapter." *The New York Times.* July 6, 2003. https://www.nytimes.com/2003/07/06/books/chapters/what-every-person-should-know-about-war.html.

[53] Vainio, Ed. *Insights of Pastoral Significance.* Lulu, 2010, p. 37.

[54] Osteen, Joel. *Your Best Life Now: 7 Steps to Living at Your Full Potential.* FaithWords, 2004.

[55] MacArthur, *Matthew 1–7.*

[56] Warren, Rick. *The Purpose Driven Life.* Zondervan, 2002.

[57] Rogers, Kenny. "The Gambler." 1978.

[58] "Reba the Landlord." *Reba.* Season 5, Ep. 17. March 17, 2006.

[59] "Statistics in the Ministry." Pastoral Care, Inc. https://www.pastoralcareinc.com/statistics/.

[60] "Statistics in the Ministry."

[61] "Reasons 18- to 22-Year-Olds Drop Out of Church." Lifeway Research. August 7, 2007. https://lifewayresearch.com/2007/08/07/reasons-18-to-22-year-olds-drop-out-of-church/.

[62] Moody, Dwight L. "February 6." *Thoughts for the Quiet Hour.* Moody Publishers, 1941.

[63] Hughes, *The Sermon on the Mount.*

[64] "The Global Religious Landscape." Pew Research Center: Religion and Public Life. December 18, 2012. https://www.pewforum.org/2012/12/18/global-religious-landscape-exec/.

[65] "World Population by Country (2013)." Worldometers. Dadax. https://www.worldometers.info/world-population/world-population-countries.php.

[66] Hackett, Conrad and David McClendon. "Christians Remain World's Largest Religious Group, but They Are Declining in Europe." Pew Research Center: Fact Tank. April 5, 2017. https://www.pewresearch.org/fact-tank/2017/04/05/christians-

remain-worlds-largest-religious-group-but-they-are-declining-in-europe/.

[67] Hackett and McClendon, "Christians Remain World's Largest Religious Group."

[68] Gilmore, James R. "170: The Sermon on the Mount." In *The Gospel History: A Complete Connected Account [of] the Life of Our Lord, Woven from the Text of the Four Evangelists.* In The Internet Archive. https://archive.org/stream/gospelhistorybei00gilm/gospelhistorybei00gilm_djvu.txt.

[69] Campolo, Tony. *It's Friday but Sunday's Comin'.* HarperCollins, 2008.

[70] MacArthur, John. *Matthew 1–28.* In *MacArthur New Testament Commentary.* Moody Publishers, 1989.

[71] Headley, Phineas Camp. *George F. Pentecost: Life, Labor, and Bible Studies.* J. H. Earle, 1880, p. 406.

[72] Hill, Jim. "What a Day." 1955. In Hymnary.org. https://hymnary.org/text/there_is_coming_a_day_when_no_heartaches.

[73] Columbus, Chris. *Hook.* Amblin Entertainment and TriStar Pictures, 1991.

www.ingramcontent.com/pod-product-compliance
Lightning Source LLC
Chambersburg PA
CBHW070805050426
42452CB00011B/1906